Discover
the Power of
Gratitude:

A GUIDE TO A
HAPPIER AND
MORE JOYFUL LIFE

Table of Contents

Introduction

Everyone endures difficult periods in their lives, and sometimes they become extremely unhappy with the cards they've been dealt. Even if you're not in a troubling situation, you could still feel something is missing from your life and chase after whatever fills this void in your heart. Maybe you're familiar with this feeling and have tried numerous solutions to resolve it. For instance, have you ever experienced a period that completely drains the life out of you? Problems keep coming at you with no end in sight. Or maybe, you've felt like this your whole life. As a result, you blame everyone and everything, never once reflecting within. However, once you do, you'll notice nothing wrong with the universe or the people you're with; the real problem stems from how you think.

Your mindset significantly influences how your world is shaped; it affects your perspective of the world and how the world treats you. Maybe you're not familiar with the concept of manifestation, or you do not believe in it. However, it is very real and very effective. If you're a pessimist, you're more likely to attract bad things and the problems you complain about. For instance, you're worried about your financial situation and expect it to worsen. It does worsen over time, and you blame the universe once again.

Now, imagine for a second that instead of negative thoughts and complaining about your financial problem, appreciate what you have in your life, like a supportive partner. You'll be more likely to attract positivity when you practice gratitude and keep a positive outlook. It will not automatically fix your financial situation, but you will feel much better when you're aware of your blessings. As a result, you'll be more motivated to fix your problems and actively look for solutions instead of giving up hope and wallowing in self-pity. This is the power of gratitude.

As a child, you're content and happy with all the little things you have. You don't have infinite desires and wants to do as an adult. Imagine feeling that way now and becoming truly happy with your life. Having a satisfied and content life is not something you need to imagine for long, as this wonderful guide to gratitude is the first step to making your dream a reality. This book teaches you how to get your simple happiness back and learn to enjoy the little moments instead of rushing through your life.

Gratitude is a choice. You can focus on the good instead of the bad. This practice doesn't have to take a lot of your time and can be incorporated as simple practices incorporated into your daily routine. If you can take 5 minutes every day for gratitude, you'll notice a wonderful change in your life. Start and end and occasionally throughout the day with gratitude.

CHAPTER 1

A Background

As an adult, most of my life was centered on my family. I was a devoted mother of four and spent plenty of time interacting with my kids. However, I remember feeling overwhelmed by the sheer amount of things I had to take care of. As a result, I did not truly appreciate the little moments of peace and joy I had with my children. I didn't realize the good I had then, and now, as time has passed, I'm becoming more aware of all the blessings the universe has bestowed upon me. I'm now a grandmother of four beautiful children, and although I had all a person could ask for, I still felt a deep uncertainty and feeling something was missing in my life. Having gone through a separation after several decades of marriage, I was now in a new phase of my life. It was an unknown phase yet equally exciting. My children were now independent, and I had more time for myself.

I started reminiscing about the past. All those days spent with my children, I didn't appreciate what was given to me. I remember sitting with my children, playing with them, and reading to them, but also overwhelmed when I looked at the mess around the house and thought of the chores I had to complete. At the time, those tasks were more important because I wanted everything to be perfect for my family. I didn't want my children to feel neglected, I didn't want my home to be a mess, and I always wanted more. Although I never failed to care for my family, I was always on the lookout for more, finding new places to go to and new things to buy for my children. I was grateful for my life then, but I didn't practice gratitude, not in the real sense anyway.

I would always say "Thank you" if I was given a compliment, a gift, or a meal, but I didn't incorporate gratitude into my daily routine, and I missed out on so much. Undoubtedly, I was immensely lucky to spend that time with my children, but I realize now I was never truly present in the moment. I was always thinking about the next thing to do, the next chore, the next activity. I never truly enjoyed the beautiful moments we shared, no matter how boring or trivial they seemed; it is a regret I will forever have. Back then, if I knew that the simple practice of gratitude would change my entire mindset and how I lived, I would've been infinitely happier during those little moments. Thankfully, I now get to share these moments with my grandchildren.

Back then, I didn't thank the universe for the beauty in the world. Now, I wake up every morning and list the things I am grateful for; it has made a world of difference in my life. I practice gratitude for all the good things that happened to me during the day every night before I sleep. Incorporating gratitude in your life can be as boring or as interesting as you want. You can thank the world for little things like having dinner on your table or for the more significant blessings like spending time with your family. Gratitude brings you more to be grateful for; it adds to your abundance. Conversely, the lack of gratitude or complaining about every problem only adds to your worries. Complainers always have something to worry about. They feel they have little good in their lives and don't enjoy the things they do have.

If you're familiar with the theory of attraction, you'd know the concept of like attracts like. How you think attracts what you get. If you have an intrinsically negative approach to life, you'll notice your problems continuously increase. The universe delivers what you believe you deserve. Many were taught to focus on what they lacked rather than appreciating what they had growing up. Most were raised in an environment that believed in scarcity, constantly reinforcing the idea that you needed more to be happy. As a result, people's lives often felt empty and unfulfilled.

Think about it. How many times have you caught yourself saying, "I'll be happy when I have that car," or "I'll finally feel content when I get that promotion?"? Conditions are placed on happiness, believing that joy can only be experienced once certain things are acquired, or specific milestones are reached. But here's the thing—the universe doesn't operate on conditional terms. When you constantly think, "I don't have…, or I won't be happy until I do," that's the message you're sending. But guess what? The universe responds by giving more of the same. You continue feeling a sense of lack, and happiness remains perpetually out of reach.

What if you shifted your perspective? Instead of dwelling on what is lacking, what if you started appreciating what you already have? What if you focused on the abundance surrounding you, no matter how small or seemingly insignificant? Gratitude is the key that unlocks this transformation. When practicing gratitude, you acknowledge your blessings, big and small. You shift your attention from scarcity to abundance, from lack to appreciation. Suddenly, your perspective broadens, and you see the beauty and richness in everyday experiences.

Gratitude is not about denying desires or becoming complacent. It's about recognizing the present moment and finding contentment. It's about being grateful for the journey, even as you strive for more. When you approach life with gratitude, you align with the universe's positive energy, inviting more blessings and joy into your life. So, break free from the cycle of lack and scarcity and embrace gratitude as a way of life.

The following chapters will take you on a journey to developing gratitude so that you can learn to love your life.

CHAPTER 2

Step 1 – Make a List

Practicing gratitude doesn't have to be complicated meditations and time-consuming activities. It can be as simple as counting your blessings. It takes no more than 5 minutes and keeps you feeling content throughout the day. So, start your day by making a list of things you're grateful for. You can do this on a piece of paper, a journal, your computer or laptop, your phone, or even in your head. You can make your list as soon as you wake up, while in the shower, or when having your morning coffee. Then, refer to this list during the day whenever you're struggling with a problem or merely need motivation. This list will remind you of the happiness of thinking about what you're grateful for.

Why is this important? Even if it's something as simple as writing a list, practicing gratitude can considerably impact your life and improve your overall well-being. When you practice this simple habit, you'll notice a clear change in your behavior. You'll feel more fulfilled, content, and motivated. Even your loved ones, friends, and peers will notice the difference in your attitude. You'll have a more relaxed demeanor, be more patient with others, and be mindful of how you treat them. A gratitude list of the people you care about will make you realize the importance of these people in your life. This list will make you wonder how different your life would be if you didn't have them or if they were to leave suddenly. It significantly alters your behavior, and you'll consciously make an effort with everything you do and everyone you come across.

For instance, imagine you've been stressed due to work issues. When you get home, your children are loud and trying to get your attention. You shout at or chastise them for their behavior and tell them to go to their room. Now, imagine yourself in the same situation, but this time, you practice gratitude. You listed your kids as one of the top things you're grateful for. You're aware of their value and know they are central to your life. When you get home, you spend time with them and listen to them when they want your attention. It doesn't mean you're not still stressed about your work; however, in this scenario, you know how much your children mean to you and how grateful you are for them. So, you treat them with love and kindness instead of being harsh and strict, making a world of difference in how your kids see you.

Reminding yourself daily of what each blessing means can considerably change your mindset and behavior, ultimately improving your life. So, how do you form this habit? Like any new practice, it's about consistency. You commit to it daily and make it a priority, like brushing your teeth or drinking coffee every morning, to become consistent with this habit. You determine how long you want to take to finish your list. You can write one in multiple ways, depending on the time you have for this activity. If you have a hard time staying consistent, consider getting an accountability buddy. Perhaps your partner could remind you or, even better, do it with you. Once you've made a few lists, note their emerging patterns. You'll likely find some activities and people that make you happy. Then try doing these activities or spending time with these people more often.

The Benefits of Making a Gratitude List

The benefits of a gratitude list are numerous, and it essentially has no cons, so why not incorporate this practice into your life? If you're still not convinced, here are some benefits practicing gratitude can bring:

1.　It Gives You Perspective

Life's not the easiest for everyone. For most people, it has many challenges and problems. Sometimes, it becomes so hard that you're completely drained of energy and feel exhausted. You could be grieving, have a serious disease, dealing with mental health issues, or struggling financially, but if you reflect on your life, you'll realize you've still got so many great things despite your problems. Making a list of these things gives you a fresh perspective on life. It doesn't allow your mind to be surrounded by negativity and reminds you of the good in your life. It makes your life worth living.

2. It Orients You

Creating several gratitude lists lets you discover what things are valuable. People usually dream about success or abundant wealth, but money and success rarely come up when they write their gratitude lists. When you write your gratitude lists, you'll realize you value different things than you thought. You might value a secondary thing more than your primary wants. For instance, maybe you think you want money, but your lists make you realize you want a break from the constant work or need a vacation. Once you're aware of your primary desires and wants, the solution might not be too difficult to find.

3. It Gives You Hope

You become hopeless when you struggle with a problem you have no solution for. Writing a gratitude list brings you hope. For instance, if you don't feel safe outside, instead of being scared and staying in your home, you realize you have the physical strength and a healthy body to develop defensive techniques. Or perhaps you're dealing with losing a loved one and feel no one could fill that void. Your gratitude list will remind you of the people that love and care for you. As a result, you will find the motivation to get better and climb out when you hit rock bottom.

4. It Reduces Stress

The human mind is a powerful machine but very vulnerable, too. If you constantly feed it negativity and sadness, that is what you'll get back. On the other hand, when you give it something that makes you happy, you'll automatically feel more content and fulfilled. A gratitude list will show you the upside to life while you deal with your challenges. Although your stress might not disappear entirely, you will feel much better than when you are obsessed over a problem you have no power over.

5. Your Gentle Reminder

Mostly, a gratitude list is your gentle reminder to enjoy the good things happening in your life. Expressing gratitude is great, but it won't matter if you don't pause, take a breath, and value the things you have. If you have legs, go for a run. If you have children, spend time with them. If you have enough money, do something you love. Enjoy all the blessings life has given you; never let your problems stop you from experiencing the joys of life because you only live once, so you might as well make the most of it.

Writing Your Gratitude List

Below are a few tips to remember when writing your gratitude list:

1. Keep It Simple

You don't have to put too much effort into your gratitude list when you're just starting out. Concise and simple will be fine. You don't need to decorate it. Focus on your handwriting, grammar, or anything else. It is merely a quick expression of what you're most grateful for.

You don't need to add a lengthy explanation; a simple sentence will do. Writing even one word is acceptable as long as you understand what it means. After all, no one else will read your lists, so you will save considerable time. Keep a journal, notebook, or paper for writing these lists. You could also opt for the notes app on your phone or download a gratitude journaling app.

2. Keep It Short

Although it depends on you, it's preferable to keep the descriptions of your items on the list short. There are no rules for gratitude journaling, but it's best to start small and move to longer descriptions with time. If your sentences are short, use bullet points or numbers to separate them.

3. Expect Increasing Specificity

When you start making these lists, you'll probably write general things you're grateful about, like your car, job, home, family, etc. However, this cannot go on too long. You can't just repeat everything on your list every other day. Make your list of topics more specific in scope, but don't rush it. Initially, you won't be aware of these small joys of life, but after practicing gratitude for a while, you'll realize all the little things that make your day. For instance, you might start writing, "I'm grateful for my children," but with time, you might write, "I'm grateful for the time I spent with my children today at the playground."

4. Write Spontaneously

Be spontaneous when writing your list, don't try to come up with descriptive explanations of things you're grateful for. Instead, let your pen naturally flow as you imagine all the good things in your life. You'll discover that the most natural inclusions in your list are those you really care about. However, there's no restriction if you need time to uncover the things you love.

5. Consider All Facets of Your Life

When making your list, express gratitude in all primary areas of your life. You can divide your list into categories and add things to each section. There's no word limit to how many things you include in each category. These categories can include but are not limited to:

- Your career
- Your friendships
- Your financial situation
- Your health and well-being
- Your romantic relationships
- Your family
- Your personal growth

6. Smile!

Smiling has many benefits. It can help you enjoy life and its simple pleasures, spread happiness and positivity to others, and relieve stress. Smiling can be genuine or forced, but both can trigger the release of endorphins in the brain. It makes you feel good because it releases endorphins, other natural painkillers, and serotonin. Together, these brain chemicals make us feel good from head to toe. Not only do they elevate your mood, but they also relax your body and reduce physical pain. It also causes the release of neurotransmitters such as dopamine and serotonin, which can boost your mood. Smiling can be contagious and create a chain reaction of smiles from person to person. So why not smile, even if you don't feel like it. Try it now!

7. Write Down What You're Grateful For

Lastly, list the things you're grateful for in your life. It could be anything, and no joy is too small to add. Even little everyday things that make you happy can be added to this list. If you're unsure where to start, consider these options and see if you can relate:

- Nutritious food
- High aspirations and progressing toward them
- Supportive friends
- Content and happy family members
- Personal growth
- A cozy and welcoming home
- Deep affection from loved ones
- Furry pets bringing you joy
- A deepening connection to spirituality
- Friendly neighbors
- Stability in financial matters
- Engaging in outdoor activities

- Pleasant weather conditions
- Possessing valuable skills, talents, and promising opportunities
- Satisfying and fulfilling career
- Enjoying relaxed conversations with friends
- Scenic and picturesque views
- Fun activities
- Maintaining composure and patience during challenging situations
- Exciting opportunities for travel
- Having leisure time to indulge in reading or listening to music
- Good physical and mental health

Starting a new hobby seems easy at first, but when you try to incorporate it into your life, you learn that staying consistent with the practice is difficult. Moreover, making gratitude lists evokes emotions when you're in a tough situation, so you could become overwhelmed or even angry. However, you should lean away from the discomfort and commit fully to this simple practice; it won't take 5 minutes of your time.

Remember to end your day with gratitude and keep smiling.

CHAPTER 3

Step 2 – A Focus Item to Prompt Your Gratitude Each Day

For the second step of your gratitude journey, start the day by writing a gratitude list. You can use some items from the previous day's list but try to add another 10 things you're grateful for. In this fast-paced world, it's pretty easy to lose sight of the simple joys of life and the numerous blessings you've been given. As an adult, you probably have a multitude of work that needs to be finished. A thousand tasks must be checked off, and numerous house chores are waiting. In this busy lifestyle, it's hard to make time for anything else or even be mindful of the present. However, if you keep going at this pace, you will miss out on so many beautiful things in this world, and soon you'll be 50 years old, lonely, and regretful of your past actions. After all, what is the purpose of life if not to enjoy the world's magnificence?

Why are you here if not to live your life to the fullest? Don't you deserve to enjoy every small happiness that comes your way? If you spend all your time stressing about the next thing, you will never appreciate or enjoy life. Gratitude will enable you to achieve your best life. The list you made at the beginning of the day is likely out of your mind by the time the sun goes down or even earlier. So, how do you remind yourself to be grateful? Through various focus items fostering gratitude and serving as a reminder to be thankful for everything you have. Looking at these items will remind you to be grateful and mindful of the present and enjoy life's minuscule niceties.

This chapter includes several ideas for creating focus items for gratitude within your life. Whether in your bedroom, bathroom, kitchen, office, or digital spaces, these reminders will bring you back to reality when you're stuck like a cog in a machine, enabling you to see the real value in life.

1. Sticky Notes

A great way to remind yourself to practice gratitude is placing sticky notes with gratitude quotes written on them all over your home. You could also write something you're grateful for on these Post-it notes and stick them to your work desk. They could go on your fridge, a wall, wardrobe, idea board, computer monitor, mirror, or even on doors so that you can catch a glimpse of them whenever you go from one room to another. As you encounter these notes, take a moment to breathe, become mindful of the present, and reflect on them.

2. Reminder Bracelet

Many people like to wear reminder bracelets if they have a bad memory or are too busy to recall something. You could get a gratitude bracelet or a pendant or charm. Whenever you see the bracelet, you'll immediately be reminded of the things you're grateful for. When you do, touch the charm, close your eyes, and express gratitude for anything you feel lucky to have at that moment. Ensure you choose a bracelet or charm that is personally significant to you. It can be a heart, a flower, or a symbol you associate with showing gratitude.

3. Gratitude Water Bottle

A gratitude water bottle might initially sound like an unconventional idea, but it's quite effective. You drink water multiple times throughout the day and possibly have a personal water bottle you keep with you wherever you go. You could get a gratitude-themed water bottle or simply attach a gratitude sticker to the one you have. When you take a sip from your bottle, you'll be reminded to practice gratitude, first for the clean drinking water you're blessed with and then for other things you immediately think of. Keeping hydrated is necessary to stay healthy, and when you connect this act with cultivating a grateful mindset, you combine two good habits into one.

4. Gratitude Journal

You can keep a gratitude journal with you throughout the day and write whatever you're grateful for whenever you are reminded of it.

For instance, if you're in your workplace and had a great meeting, you feel confident and super grateful for being given the opportunity of a lifetime. So, you jot down how you're feeling immediately into your gratitude journal. It saves a cherished memory for you, which you can later read and recall the feeling. Ensure this journal is compact so it's easy to carry. Gratitude journaling will be discussed in detail in the next chapter.

5. Gratitude Rock or Pebble

This method is tactile or sensory therapy activated through touch. Although it is usually done to treat mental disorders, it often helps people with memory recall. Find a smooth, medium-sized rock or pebble that fits comfortably in your hands and pocket. It must not be too heavy since you'll carry it around most of the day. Whenever you put your hand in your pocket, you'll touch the rock and instantly be reminded of your gratitude practice. It is a physical reminder to be grateful throughout the day. Even if it doesn't happen naturally, reach into your pocket whenever you're free during the day, like when waiting in line, commuting, or taking a break. When you do, acknowledge the present moment, count your blessings, and express gratitude. You could count the blessings you can see, feel, or hear in the moment; this will encourage your mindfulness practice.

6. Inspirational Quotes or Affirmation Cards

There's nothing better than inspirational quotes to remind you of the transformative power of gratitude. You could make affirmation cards and place them throughout the house to be reminded of all the good in your life. You can print or write them down with pretty colored markers. You could even get these framed and hang them on your bedroom wall. Or put them on your study or work desk. When you see these positive affirmations or inspirational reminders, reflect on what they're highlighting.

You can design them as flashcards and keep a different card with you every day. For instance, perhaps you're having problems with your job. Take a card that helps you get through them. It could be, "I am grateful for my job because it helps put a roof over my head, food in my stomach, and lets me be independent to do the things I enjoy." Whenever you feel overwhelmed, and the negative thoughts are coming, read your affirmation card, and you'll feel considerably better.

Here are some inspirational quotes you may enjoy:

- *"Gratitude unlocks the fullness of life. It turns what we have into enough and more. It turns denial into acceptance, chaos into order, and confusion into clarity."* - Melody Beattie
- *"Gratitude is not only the greatest of virtues but the parent of all others."* - Marcus Tullius Cicero
- *"When you are grateful, fear disappears, and abundance appears."* - Anthony Robbins
- *"Gratitude makes sense of our past, brings peace for today, and creates a vision for tomorrow."* - Melody Beattie

- *"Gratitude is a powerful catalyst for happiness. It's the spark that lights a fire of joy in your soul."* - Amy Collette
- *"The more grateful I am, the more beauty I see."* - Mary Davis
- *"Gratitude is the fairest blossom which springs from the soul."* - Henry Ward Beecher
- *"Gratitude is the healthiest of all human emotions. The more you express gratitude for what you have, the more likely you will have even more to express gratitude for."* - Zig Ziglar
- *"Gratitude can transform common days into thanksgivings, turn routine jobs into joy, and change ordinary opportunities into blessings."* - William Arthur Ward
- *"Gratitude is the wine for the soul. Go on. Get drunk."* - Rumi
- *"The more you practice the art of thankfulness, the more you have to be thankful for."* - Norman Vincent Peale

Also, here are some affirmations you might like:

- I am grateful for the abundance of love and support in my life
- I appreciate the beauty surrounding me every day
- I am thankful for the opportunities that come my way, both big and small
- I am blessed with good health and a body that allows me to experience life fully

- I am grateful for the relationships in my life that bring joy and fulfillment
- I appreciate the simple pleasures bringing me happiness
- I am thankful for the lessons I've learned from successes and challenges
- I am grateful for the peace and tranquility I find within myself
- I appreciate the wonders of nature and the harmony it brings to my soul
- I am thankful for the present moment and the infinite possibilities it holds

7. Mindful Jewelry

Wearing pieces of jewelry that remind you to practice gratitude or mindfulness can be quite effective when trying to practice gratitude throughout the day consistently. It is a tactile therapy because you are instantly reminded of gratitude when you unconsciously touch the piece of jewelry. Use a necklace, pendant, or even a small charm you can connect to a keychain. When you need to ground yourself in the present moment, reach out for this piece of jewelry. As you observe the texture, weight, and shape of the piece, take a few deep breaths, and think about something you're grateful for at that moment.

8. Gratitude Bell or Wind Chime

This method is sound therapy or recall, making you consciously develop a habit of practicing gratitude when you hear a certain sound

- in this case, a bell sound or wind chimes. Attach the bell or wind chimes near a window or door so it catches your attention easily. This way, the sounds will remind you to pause, breathe, and be grateful. Let the soft sound of the bells be your cue to shift your focus from whatever's bothering you to things you're thankful for.

9. Gratitude Jar

A gratitude jar is another great activity to incorporate gratitude into your life and practice daily. A gratitude jar can be as simple as a basic container labeled "Gratitude Jar," or you can decorate it. Next to the jar, place pieces of paper on which you can write what you're grateful for at that moment. Ensure you place this setup in a prominent place in your house, like your work desk or kitchen counter. When you notice the jar, take a pen and piece of paper, write down your blessing, and put it into the jar. At the end of the day or week, depending on the number of chits you've put in, go through them. You could ask your family members or roommates to participate with you. It will likely make you more consistent with the activity.

10. Gratitude Wallpaper

If you often work on your laptop or PC or have a habit of opening your phone frequently, set a gratitude practice wallpaper on them. You can select an image, a quote, or artwork that resonates with you and makes you feel blessed. It could be a picture of your family with quotes or affirmations. Every time you unlock your phone or start your laptop, you'll see this reminder and feel grateful.

Practicing gratitude does not have to be hard work, multiple practices, and time-consuming activities. All you need is to incorporate little habits into your life, reminding you to be grateful and present at the moment. You can try any focus items in this chapter to remind you to practice gratitude or incorporate them all into your life. When you notice these little reminders everywhere, you'll undoubtedly not miss this practice, even for a day.

Remember to end your day with gratitude and keep smiling.

CHAPTER 4

Step 3 - End Your Day with Gratitude

For the third step of your gratitude practice, make another list of things you're grateful for at the beginning of your day. You can continue writing from where you left off the day before or start a new one. Try to add at least 10 new things you're thankful for. Also, incorporate all the focus items discussed in the previous chapter to keep practicing gratitude throughout the day. When your day comes to an end, practice a few final gratitude techniques to end your day on a good note. Look back at your day and think about all the good things that happened. You can make a mental list of everything you're grateful for while doing your bedtime routines, like brushing your teeth, skincare, making your bed, or taking your dog outside.

At the end of the day, you're often tired and drained. You just want to hit the bed and leave this world behind as you drift off to sleep.

Focusing on the good is especially difficult when you've had a hard day. However, when you practice gratitude before bed, you become aware of the good things that happened in your day, even if they were small. For instance, maybe your boss yelled at you after you ruined your presentation, and it has been on your mind all day. However, when you consider every detail of the day, you will be joyful when you realize your coworker defended you, taking some of the blame off you.

You will find numerous similar occurrences that will bring you comfort, even after a bad day. Therefore, nightly gratitude routines are considered very effective. This chapter includes two common gratitude practices you can try before bed - gratitude journaling and guided meditation. Both techniques are incredibly effective, especially when trying to incorporate gratitude into your life.

Gratitude Journaling

Many believe that gratitude journals resemble teenage diaries. In actuality, you don't really write about the events of your day as much as it's a chance to write about what you're grateful for. Although there are many templates and guides for writing a gratitude journal, everyone has a unique writing style. Some people simply write about their day, highlighting the good parts. Others choose a specific part of their life they're grateful for. You should try gratitude journaling before bed and write about your blessings for the day. Before you start writing, here are some tips you should consider:

1. Choose a Journal

Since you're planning to make journaling a habit, getting a new gratitude journal makes sense. When selecting a new journal, you must consider several factors. Would you prefer a physical journal, or would a digital one suffice? Will you keep the journal on your person or store it in your room? How do you want the style and template to be? Traditional journals are the best for several reasons. First, they're durable and affordable; second, there's a unique charm of writing in a traditional journal that digital journals cannot provide. However, they do cost almost nothing online. So, if you don't have the means to buy a new journal or are too lazy to get one, you can always start with a digital journal. A new journal is precisely what you need to be inspired and started.

2. Set Aside Time for Writing

At first, it'll be challenging to make time for this habit, especially at night when you're completely drained. This activity might even feel like adding another thing to your endless To-do list. However, once you get into the habit of writing in your gratitude journal every night, you'll realize the initial effort was worth it. Maybe you could combine it with an existing habit, like reading before bed. It will automatically create time for writing. Remember, with journaling, consistency is key. If you skip days, you'll avoid the task every other day until you completely give up on this good habit. When you journal regularly, you'll see true change in your life.

3.   **Start with Gratitude Journal Prompts**

When you're just starting with journaling, coming up with what you want to write can be daunting. You can use these general prompts to get started and then adapt them to suit:

- Write three funny things your kids did today
- Write about a time you were grateful for someone after they did something for you
- Write about the many ways you can thank someone without uttering the words 'thank you.'
- Consider the work that went into the clothes you wear or your house
- Write about a time you were grateful for something a loved one did for you
- What's something you believe makes you unique?
- Take a peek outside the window, and write about what you see that you're grateful for
- What would you save if you had to get rid of your things?
- Write about anything current in your life that you didn't have a year ago.
- Write about something you're looking forward to.
- Write yourself a sweet thank you note
- Remember a time you laughed so hard that you cried.
- Flip through the photos on your cellphone and choose a random photo. Write about what this photo makes you feel and why you're grateful.

- Remember a mistake you made and write about the lesson you learned from it. Mention why you're grateful for this learning experience.
- Remember four different situations that made you smile this week.
- Has anyone shaped who you are today? Write about them and why you're grateful that you have this person in your life.
- List two people who have supported and helped you through a difficult time in your life.
- Think about the times you have helped people, and write about it
- Name someone who did something nice for you this week

4. Think of Fresh Topics

While consistently journaling will get you practicing gratitude regularly, you might come up short of topics to write about after a while. If you've written about something already, view it from a different angle, and you'll come up with entirely new material. For instance, if you've previously written about how grateful you are for your partner, you can view them from someone else's perspective and then write about their qualities. Remember, you can write about anything, no matter how big or small. There are no rules when it comes to journaling. It is an activity entirely for you. If you're at a loss about what to write, here are some unique journal ideas to help you get inspired:

People to write about:

- Someone you haven't spoken to in a long time
- Your child's teacher
- Someone you don't get along with
- Someone who lives far away but means a lot to you
- A musician, artist, or author who inspires you
- A stranger who made your day better
- Your coworkers

Things to write about:

- The cup of morning coffee you savor upon waking up
- The food that tops your list of favorites
- Everyday items you rely on
- Your career
- Enjoyable pastimes and hobbies
- Your body
- Your senses of smell, sight, taste, and more

Places to write about:

- The vibrant place you call home
- The dreamy vacation spot you love the most
- Your dedicated workstation at the office
- The cozy haven of your bed
- The serene park in your neighborhood
- The cherished place you grew up in
- The beloved bookstore that captures your heart

Ideas to write about:

- A cherished family tradition
- A lighthearted and humorous moment
- A personal struggle you are facing
- A recent change in your life
- An accomplishment you recently achieved
- The current season of the year
- Something new you have recently learned

5. Find What Works for You

The best part of free journaling is there are no rules; you can write anything that works for you since it's for your eyes only. So, you can make it all about your interests and what you enjoy. If you love to doodle, get an unlined journal, and draw sketches with your entries. Do you prefer visuals but aren't a great artist? You can always get photos printed and attach them to your journal. Your journal can be anything you choose; a sketchbook-gratitude journal or a scrapbook-journal hybrid. Consider involving your partner or kids when you become more comfortable with your writing. When eating dinner after a long day, go around the table, allowing everyone to share what they're grateful for. Or you can make this a part of your bedtime routine when you're tucking the kids in. It will be great practice for your family and keep you accountable for practicing gratitude every night.

Once you know how to start with this practice, you'll be on your way to a successful gratitude journaling journey. When you reflect on the things you're grateful for, you'll automatically express your gratitude to others. You'll be more appreciative of your loved ones, friends, family, and others you're grateful for. Remember, do not get discouraged when starting out on this journey; it's okay to struggle with consistency. It takes time to create a new habit, so it's completely understandable if you struggle initially.

Guided Meditation for Gratitude

To begin gratitude meditation, find a comfortable seat, allowing your eyes to remain closed or softly gaze ahead. Ensure you sit in a comfortable position and maintain a straight spine for optimal balance. Feel free to sway gently back and forth or side to side until you discover your ideal seat. Allow your body to settle into this position.

Take a few slow breaths, releasing the desire to control or manipulate your breath. Let it flow naturally, entering and leaving your body effortlessly. Relax and let go of tension or stress, cultivating relaxed alertness and grounding in the present moment.

Become aware. Observe your state of mind. What is your prevailing mood? How do you feel right now? Practice simple observation without passing judgment or categorizing it as good or bad.

Now, shift your focus to acknowledging and appreciating everything you are grateful for. Feel gratitude for the people and circumstances that have brought you to this moment today. Extend gratitude to your parents and grandparents. Appreciate the opportunities you have been blessed with in education, travel, and work experiences.

Consider the well-being of your mind and body. Express gratitude for your body's health. Feel grateful for the faculties of your mind and intellect. Appreciate the talents and skills you possess. Now, reflect on the people in your life and express gratitude for their presence. Show appreciation to your immediate and extended family. Extend your gratitude to your coworkers, friends, and mentors who have contributed to your personal growth and development.

Direct your gratitude toward the Earth, the source of life. Express appreciation for water, food, and the air you breathe. Lastly, choose one thing you feel exceptionally grateful for at this moment. Allow every muscle in your body to relax completely.

Delve deeper into the experience of gratitude through brief visualization. Bring to mind someone you deeply care for—a parent, spouse, child, or close friend. Visualize them in your mind's eye and recall a moment when you felt an intense connection with this person. It could be a recent or past memory. Allow your mind to revisit this sacred moment of connection. Recall the surroundings, the location, the people present, and the time of day, visualizing every detail.

Attempt to rekindle the emotions you felt during that moment—love, presence, contentment, or a true connection. Notice the sensations or emotions that arise within your mind and body, letting go of judgments or analyses. Simply allow these feelings to come and go freely.

Focus on one specific aspect of this cherished moment you feel particularly grateful for. It could be the person, the setting, or your emotional state. Let this experience of gratitude envelop your entire being—mind and body. Take a few more breaths maintaining your focus on this quality of gratitude.

Now, reinforce the benefits of this gratitude meditation. Deliberately pause for 15 seconds to savor this experience of gratitude. Allow it to penetrate your being deeply. When you're ready, open your eyes and slowly return to the present. Move the parts of your body that feel stiff or tense.

As you continue the rest of your day, consider expressing your appreciation to the person you visualized during this practice. You can send them a text, an email, or a card or offer them a mental wish of gratitude. Observe how this expression of gratitude influences the rest of your day.

Ending the day with a guided meditation or cathartic gratitude journaling will make a world of difference in your behavior. As you consciously redirect your focus toward gratitude, you will empower yourself to embrace the positive aspects of your life and let go of negativity. These simple yet profound acts of self-reflection and appreciation pave the way for a more peaceful and fulfilling existence. Engaging in guided meditation allows you to cultivate inner calm, releasing accumulated stress or tension from the day.

Remember to end your day with gratitude and keep smiling.

CHAPTER 5

Step 4 - Family

"Other things may change us, but we start and end with family."
-Anthony Brandt

Family can be a controversial topic to tackle. But what defines the word family? They can be the people you were born, raised, and lived with. The ones you open presents on Christmas with, fight with on Thanksgiving, and light up the sky with on the 4th of July. They're the blood relations. But at other times, they're not. Instead, they are the people who cared about you when your flesh and blood didn't.

They are your closest relatives. However, families are known to come with hardships, and as much as I'd love to agree with dear Anthony Brandt, they have their fair share of drama. Sometimes, these dramas can become tricky to be thankful for when they're around. During hardships and discord, it's common for people to want to cut ties and run away. Without a doubt, some find it hard to be grateful for their existence.

Families come in all shapes and sizes; it can be big with all the members around or a simple household of a single mother and son. If you are blessed with a happy and understanding family, the following tips and tricks should be easy. If you struggle with being on the same page with your next of kin, by the end of this, you should understand your emotions toward them and appreciate their existence.

Why You Should Be Grateful for Having a Family

Some people struggle to find a reason to reconnect or maintain a strong connection with their closest relatives, whether those you didn't choose (father, mother, siblings, aunts, and cousins) or those you do choose to be with (spouse and their extended family, dear friends, Godparents of your children). So, why should you bother and make an effort?

You're Here

You're here so you might as well make the best of it. You're reading a guide on how to be and feel better and working to improve your social skills with the people closest to you; it's evidence of love, nourishment, and care. You care about your and others' emotional well-being, which shows emotional intelligence. You are on the precipice of a journey to better yourself and sustain healthy relationships for a brighter future.

Learning to be grateful for your family aids in your ascension mentally and emotionally and assists in casting away built-up negative emotions.

A Backbone

During great life disappointments, for example, bereavement, job loss, sickness, or monetary challenges, people often look to those who provide comfort. Family is a strong source of mental and emotional support. They have your back and are ready to stand by you and, in some cases, face your hardships with you. They push you forward to be better and carry on in the darkest times.

Family is ready to lend a hand, whether financially or physically, or simply to drive for miles to give you a shoulder to lean on. No matter how dark or distant you become, coming back together is never easier when you're in need.

Shared Experiences

Coming from a broken family, divorced, or separated parents, or a deceased member within the immediate circle is common. These experiences, or, in some cases, traumas, allow growth. Yes, they are extremely painful and traumatic, and most would prefer not to experience them. Nonetheless, they make you stronger, bonding the remaining family together. Through the trials of your closest relationships, you are taught what works and what doesn't. Use the interactions as reflections on what within you needs healing, what needs to be embraced, and what you need to set aside.

By practicing gratitude for your family, you're repairing wounds you might not have known were there, preventing their occurrence in the next generation.

History

You share the most memories with the people you grew up with. You have the same roots and have been together through countless good and bad times. You are shaped from the same mold - someone to share a unique perspective on the world with, funny stories, and exclusive traditions, further bonding the family together.

In trying times, it helps to have someone who's been through it with you to understand where you're coming from and offer comfort and pragmatic advice.

Consistent

They know you best. If you're sad, your mother knows to cook your favorite meal. If you're fighting, they'll still do your laundry. If you're having a hard time, they'll bring you groceries. If you're feeling down, they'll know the right words to lift you up and remind you of the triumphs they were blessed to witness. They cheer you on when you think you can't make it. You know you can rely on them for these simple favors because it makes their existence a reason for being thankful.

They Endure You

No one is an angel. Everyone has ups and downs and sideways. Sometimes it's hard for someone who hasn't seen you on your best and worst days to accept you as you are.

Your family knows most of your dirty secrets, the things you are ashamed of, the trouble you got into, and the bodies they buried with you. They stick around through thick and thin. They can mock and tell jokes at your expense, but if someone else does it, they better run.

They know you inside and out, and no matter what, they stay by your side when no one else will.

Reasons to Be Grateful for Your Family

Make a point to be grateful for the simple and small things your family offers you. Create a list of everything that comes to mind. Peruse it every day and add to it if you've forgotten something. These lists act as an alarm triggering the brain into more positive associations with your family members. Write down all the good attributes of each member; more will come to mind later. In time fondness will replace the negative emotions normally associated with that person.

A good way of creating these lists is saying, *"I am Grateful for...."* Or *"I am thankful for ...."*

Listed below are a few examples to get you started on your list:

- I am grateful I can rely on you to lift my spirits when they're low
- I am grateful to always have different people willing to listen to me
- I am grateful that no matter what, you cheer me on to keep going
- I am grateful you love me unconditionally
- I am grateful I can count on you to take care of me when I'm sick
- I am grateful for all the meals you so lovingly prepared for me
- I am grateful you could forgive me for things no one else would
- I am grateful for having default secret keepers
- I am grateful to have someone who knows me inside and out
- I am grateful for all the surprises you gave me
- I am grateful for your support in all my endeavors
- I am grateful for having natural friends sharing the same blood
- I am grateful for your company and companionship
- I am grateful you always think the best of me
- I am grateful you always help me point north
- I am grateful for all the laughs we shared and continue to share

- I am grateful for the memories, holidays, and gatherings that were full of fun
- I am grateful you supported my decisions even when they seemed wrong to you
- I am grateful you were there for me through hardships
- I am grateful for everything you taught me
- I am grateful you never judged me and accepted me as I am
- I am grateful I can be myself without pretending around you
- I am grateful for my biggest cheerleaders
- I am grateful for all the times you drove me around
- I am grateful for the love you shower me with
- I am grateful for the thousand kisses and hugs that made me feel better
- I am grateful for the shared experiences and inside jokes no one else understands
- I am grateful you taught me how to face life on my own

You can use the above list however you like. You can specify events from your past or make the message specific to one person. Play around with it however you like until you reach the format that adds the most value.

Healing as a Family through Gratitude

One of the easiest ways to express gratitude toward someone is to come out straight and say it. Through this expression, the other person feels valued, loved, and appreciated, and their positivity reflects on you. By sharing the positive experience, the action will likely reoccur, starting a cycle of kindness and strengthening family bonds.

A family can express gratitude and be encouraged as a unit in several ways:

Generating Opportunities to Express Gratitude

Being thankful is not easy during hardships or when things don't go your way. Therefore, focusing on the small, good moments during trying times to relieve stress is important.

For example, simple gestures like the following:

- Always using courteous language like please and thank you, can go a long way
- Recognizing efforts made to improve a skill or have a more positive attitude
- Suggest that each person voice something they are thankful for during small gatherings, car rides, or meals.
- Write notes of endearment or encouragement to each other

Journaling

Journaling specific to gratitude is a healing method implemented by many mental health specialists. It trains the brain to find the good things around it and reminds it to be thankful daily. When done as a family, the journal could include things other family members performed you are thankful for. It could be something that happened in the presence of a family member that made you grateful. Or the simple daily things that make you happy.

To encourage journaling, some families share points of gratitude weekly. They create incentives to ensure the action remains consistent. For example, they can be small rewards following the completion of a week of journaling.

Games

Making gratitude practice fun can cement it in the nervous system. It helps the bonding between family members when performed together.

For instance, take turns saying what you're grateful for using the alphabet. As you move forward in the letters, it becomes more challenging and fun.

Read

Introduce books about gratitude to your household. You can read books examining what-if scenarios or different circumstances. Sometimes the only way people express thankfulness is after learning about someone else's worse experiences.

For children, you can find a multitude of choices to pick from, like Grumpy Ninja by Mary Nhin or Brave Girl: Clara and the shirtwaist makers strike of 1909 by Michelle Markle.

Bedtime Gratitude

Bedtime gratitude is a practice that usually works best with younger children but is worth a try with older ones.

The aim is to imbed gratitude practices at bedtime by reciting three good things that happened during the day. It gives the child a sense of serenity as they drift off to sleep and prepares them for the next day with a more positive outlook.

You can perform the same practice yourself by writing in a journal or repeating the things you're thankful for in your mind as you doze off.

Acknowledging the Negative Experiences

This might seem like a contradiction to what came before. However, it is important to refrain from dismissing negative emotions; it only allows them to build up. When emotions are openly expressed, it makes them easier to deal with.

You can alter the bedtime routine slightly by expressing these negative emotions at dinner instead of immediately before sleep.

Remember, it doesn't always have to be negative experiences. You can divide your proclamation into three parts. First, something you're thankful for. Second, something that wasn't pleasant. Third, something you hope will happen. This way, you create a balance without skewing one way or the other.

Families do not have to be blood-related. But whoever you regard as family, always show gratitude, love, and appreciation toward them.

Remember to end your day with gratitude and keep smiling.

CHAPTER 6

Step 5- Relationships

In the song "Eleanor Rigby," the Beatles asked, "All the lonely people, where do they all come from?" It is an interesting question. Although there are billions of people around the world, many can't shake the feeling they are alone or don't belong. Even those on social media who have an active social life and many friends can feel lonely. The answer is simple, strong and quality relationships are hard to find.

A loving partner or a supportive friend is a blessing many people take for granted. You are lucky if you have someone you can call at any time during the day to talk about your problems, and they listen without judgment.

Sometimes it can be hard to think fondly of people who once played a big role in your life, like a former best friend or ex-spouse, especially if you ended things on bad terms. However, you might not realize it now, but these people have taught you a lesson or changed your life significantly. So, remember them with gratitude rather than resentment.

All relationships are precious; today, be thankful for all the great people in your life.

The Importance of Relationships in Your Life

If you mostly feel happy and uplifted, look at the company you keep. You most likely have supportive friends, partners, and family who bring joy into your life. Healthy relationships can substantially impact your life. You will be less stressed, more satisfied, more confident, and more eager to take risks and try new things.

However, if you don't have people you can count on, you will feel numb, sad, angry, and alone. Your life won't function how you want it to, your needs won't be met, and you will always feel your life is falling apart.

Life is filled with hardships and heartbreaks. You need your loved ones by your side to hold you when you are crying, remind you of how amazing you are whenever you lose faith in yourself, and give you hope when things aren't going your way.

Why You Should Be Grateful for Your Relationships

Unfortunately, many people aren't aware of how lucky they are to have a support system. They realize how this person touched their lives only after they lose someone special.

Close your eyes and think of the last time you had a bad day. Was there someone by your side? Would you have gotten through it without this person? How different would your life be if they didn't come through for you?

Nowadays, many people complain rather than appreciate. How many times have you complained to your friends about your partner? When was the last time you had a fight with your best friend over something they didn't do instead of thanking them for all the times they were there for you? Don't feel guilty. You aren't alone. It is always easier to focus on the bad when you don't regularly practice gratitude.

Sometimes, you focus on other people's relationships and think they have it better than you. However, if you constantly express your gratitude for your loved ones, you will realize you have it as good, if not better.

So, take this opportunity today to think of all the amazing people in your life and how they've made it better, and be grateful they exist. Once you remember all the wonderful things they do for you, you will appreciate them more.

You could send them a message or call them to thank them for being there for you over the years. As a result, they will feel happy and appreciated and express their gratitude for you, strengthening your relationship.

Be Grateful for Your Partner

If you have a partner, be grateful for them. Maybe you don't always see eye to eye, but generally, they support you and help you around the house and with the children. Think of your special moments and all the good things they do for you, and express gratitude for them.

Here are a few examples of expressing gratitude for your partner:

- I am grateful for your unmatched sense of humor and for making me laugh so hard every day
- I remember every time I get sick; you will leave everything behind to be by my side and take care of me
- Whenever we want to order takeout, you always suggest my favorite restaurant even though you don't like their food
- Whenever I tell you I am having a bad day, you rush to be by my side and find ways to make me laugh
- I love your ambition and hard-working personality that pushes you to realize your dreams
- Thank you for being loving, kind, and patient with our children

- Thank you for teaching our children to be responsible
- I am grateful that you push and encourage me to work harder on myself and achieve my goals
- I love how you respect and appreciate my family
- Your nice compliments never fail to put a smile on my face
- Thank you for tolerating me when I am not pleasant or when I make it difficult to be around me
- Thank you for listening to everything I say, even when I talk about silly things
- Thank you for understanding me better than I understand myself
- I am grateful you always find ways to make me smile
- I am so thankful for your kindness and patience with me, even when we don't see eye to eye
- It makes me happy that you always find ways to make it up to me when we fight
- Thank you for forgiving me when I say something I don't mean or do something regrettable
- Thank you for accepting my flaws and never trying to change me
- I am so grateful for your honesty and for trusting me with all your secrets
- Thank you for your loyalty and for never giving me a reason to doubt you
- I love how you are my biggest cheerleader

- Thank you for all the small gestures you make to show me I am always on your mind, like the good morning texts you send me every day
- I am grateful for your positive influence on me
- I can be my unapologetic self around you, and you never judge me
- I am home around you. You make me comfortable and carefree like a child
- I love how you remember every tiny detail about me, even those I forget
- Whenever I am sad, you always find ways to make me smile
- Thank you for never giving up on us, even on our worst days, and loving me even when I can be unlovable
- I am grateful that you always have my back
- Thank you for making our lives a beautiful, fun, and exciting adventure
- Thank you for making me believe in true love

Be Grateful for Your Friendships

Friends are the family you choose. They can enrich your life and make it better in every way. They always pull you up when you fall apart and are the first ones to celebrate your successes and joy. Good friends provide emotional support when you need it and help you adapt to new situations. Whenever you doubt yourself, they will cheer on you and remind you of all your good qualities.

Not all friends are the same. Some you see all the time and can rely on them to come to your aid whenever you need them. Others might be distant, but you know they are good for a catch-up or chat. You should cherish and be grateful for all of them.

Here are a few examples of expressing gratitude for your friends:

- Thank you for all the great advice you give me, even when I am being stubborn and difficult
- I am grateful you call me out whenever I make a dumb mistake and never hesitate to tell me the truth, even if it hurts, because you know it's for my own good
- I am thankful for all the times you made me laugh so hard that tears ran from my eyes
- I am grateful for all the times you made ordinary moments extraordinary
- I am grateful for the long nights you spent with me on the phone, listening to me talk about the same problem over and over. You are patient and understanding and help me get through the tough times
- I am grateful for every time we disagree and you meet me halfway
- Thank you for never asking me to sacrifice my happiness, dreams, or relationships for our friendship because you understand that I am sometimes very busy
- I am grateful for your compassion and kindness
- It makes me happy how you always find time for me
- Thank you for keeping your promises

- It always warms my heart that you can sense I am sad from the tone of my voice or just by looking into my eyes
- Thank you for apologizing each time you are wrong and admitting your mistakes
- I am grateful for your support when I follow my heart or make questionable decisions
- Thank you for never saying, "I told you so."
- Thank you for sticking with me through the good and bad times
- I am thankful for you standing up for me and being my strength when I am weak
- I am grateful you make my problems "our problems."
- I am happy you are always there for me because you want to and don't have to, and you never make me feel like a burden
- I am grateful you believe in me even when I don't believe in myself
- Thank you for making me feel valued
- Thank you for loving me without wanting anything in return
- I am grateful you always find it in your heart to forgive me and never hold grudges
- I am thankful you never invade my space and give me alone time whenever I need it
- Thank you for answering when I call

- I am grateful that even though we don't see or talk with each other for months or years, I never feel things between us can ever change
- Thank you for being you and making my life better

Be Grateful for People from Your Past

Every person that comes into your life has a purpose. Maybe they are meant to teach you a lesson or push you to change certain things in your life. For instance, a bad friend can teach you not to trust people immediately, or an ex-partner can show you what you don't need in a relationship.

Rather than feeling bitter toward an ex-partner, remember how, at one stage, there was something about that person you were drawn to and loved. If you can feel a small amount of gratitude for that person, you will feel less bitterness and more happiness.

It hurts when you are estranged from a sibling, parent, or friend. However, if you think back to before the falling out, you will find at least three things you are grateful to that person for. Maybe they played games with you, or you walked to school together when you were young. They could have helped you get your first job or introduced you to your partner. You don't have to act to heal the relationship, but if you feel gratitude for a few small things, your anger toward that person will significantly reduce.

Here are a few examples of expressing gratitude for people from your past:

- I am grateful for the memories we once shared
- I am thankful for the love you gave me
- Thank you for teaching me a valuable lesson
- I am grateful I have learned to love myself and don't need another person's validation
- Thank you for being a part of my childhood
- I am thankful for all the laughter and the tears we shared
- Thank you for showing me I can love someone with all my heart
- I am happy remembering the times you helped or provided me with a shoulder to cry on and arms to hold me
- I am grateful for all the things you did for me

All your relationships matter. Be grateful for all the people who touched your life in one way or another. Tell them how much they mean to you and how lucky you are to have met them. Release the ones who no longer walk your path and think of them fondly.

Remember to end your day with gratitude and keep smiling.

CHAPTER 7

Step 6 – Health and Body

On this day, you can show gratitude for one of the greatest gifts you'll ever have, your body. Being grateful for the great machine - your body and health - is a fantastic way to boost your mood. Moreover, by appreciating your body, you're becoming healthier. Whether you're battling an illness or have physical deficits due to a past condition, it doesn't matter. What matters is appreciating what you have and making the best of it for a happier life.

The Importance of Being Grateful for Your Body and Health

When did you last think about your body and were grateful for it? Throughout your life, you probably looked in the mirror and wished one or more parts of your body were different. Perhaps, it was your height, weight, or the little imperfections that make you unique. During these moments, you never stop to think that whatever your body looks like, it keeps you alive, happy and healthy. Practicing expressing gratitude for your body and health, you will look in the mirror and be happy with what you see because you'll know that without your body sustaining your health and happiness, none of it would matter anyway.

Reflect on when you were sick recently. Whether a stomach bug or a serious illness that you landed up in a hospital, all you wanted was to feel better. Fortunately, the complex mechanism of your body stepped in and - with some help from medicine - repaired your ailment, restoring your health. It might have got you through surgery or grueling physical therapy. Your pain and the fatigue from the illness that depletes your body of energy made it hard to remember you were once healthy. In these moments, people realize they take their health for granted. Instead, they should be thankful for their health when and while they have it.

As you reflect on your body, know that many are battling an illness or lost a sense, or a part of their body. Perhaps, one of your friends or family members has recently been diagnosed with cancer. If you're fortunate enough to be free of these life-threatening concerns, it should be all the more reason to be grateful for your health and body. Even if you've lost a sensory or body part due to illness or an accident, it doesn't signify not having much to appreciate. For example, if you have lost your hearing, focus on being thankful that you have your eyesight and vice versa. If you have lost a limb, be grateful someone invented a prosthesis to allow you to be independently mobile.

Perhaps a couple of days before you became ill or injured due to an accident, you were unsatisfied with a workout performance and pushed your body more. Or, you might be disappointed because you skipped a workout day, making you believe you'll never achieve your goals. Yet when you felt poorly, none of it mattered.

When was the last time you appreciated having had a good night's sleep? Perhaps you take your body for granted, even knowing you can function with less than optimal sleep. For instance, those nights you spend anticipating a stressful day at work or a difficult conversation with a friend or family member instead of getting enough sleep. Practicing gratitude for your body makes you appreciate the energy you have the next day.

When you have time to be physically active, do you feel grateful for how your body makes it possible? Or, are you too busy counting steps and calories on your smartwatch, taking pictures with your phone, or having a silent fictional conversation in your mind? If these sound familiar, know you aren't alone. Too many people go about their day barely noticing what their body does to allow them to spend their days without or with as few limitations as possible.

What Does It Mean to Be Grateful for Your Health?

The meaning of gratitude for your health differs from one person to another. It is appreciating your body and health by being grateful for being alive. For many, this translates to being appreciative of the abilities facilitated by their health, physically and mentally. Gratitude for your health can also denote your confidence in knowing that you can adapt to various conditions when plans change or travel to a place experiencing all you can. Traveling and knowing you can accommodate any circumstance you encounter is a luxury many people don't have. If you do, saying thanks for the blessing will make you appreciate it even more.

Being thankful for your health gives you the freedom of not being afraid that you won't accomplish something or hurt yourself while trying. Imagine living on the fifth floor and having to walk up the stairs because the elevator is broken. Being grateful is thanking your legs for carrying you, your body for cooperating, and your lungs for supporting you without exploding.

Honoring your health gives you the confidence to have the power to move all the things you pick up during the day, take care of your pets and kids, manage your home, and have enough energy to do something you enjoy every day. Simultaneously, appreciate your health and recognize the more advanced concept of health.

What Is Health?

Most people define health as the absence of disease symptoms and other health conditions and the presence of vitality, which fuels the body and mind with energy. However, if being thankful for something is honoring and praising it, wouldn't you want to acknowledge every part of your health and body which allows you to be who you are? If you only appreciate that you aren't sick and have enough energy, you're taking the rest of your health for granted, not to mention the body that fuels your health.

Since gratitude is a learned practice, needing more time to learn how to honor your health is entirely normal. Finding time to show gratitude for your health can be challenging if you have a busy life.

Some people refuse to explore the deepest layers of gratitude for health by not paying attention to their body or mind. Or if they do, they only see imperfections and be hypervigilant of changes, like weight gain or loss, the appearance of a wrinkle, etc. Their behavior might be driven by prolonged stress, traumatic experiences, or other circumstances causing the distorted reality. Those who don't care about their health will camouflage their thoughts with other activities. Conversely, overly focused people will see their body as something to be molded, pushed to the limit, or reprieved of nourishment, instead of the mechanism that sustains their life.

When you let yourselves fully appreciate your health, you develop capacities to find joy in the little things. Praising your health means showing gratitude for feeling the sun's warmth on your back, the revitalizing boost you get after a nap, the sensation you get when your loved one touches you, the joy recalling memories bring, and overall health and well-being. Think of your body and how it works, and be grateful you're alive. Remember, always end your day with gratitude and keep smiling.

Reasons to Be Grateful for Your Health

It Allows You to Spend Time with Your Loved Ones

There is no better cure for feeling down than spending time with people who bring you happiness and joy. Surrounding yourself with loved ones reduces anxiety and depression. Being healthy allows you to spend as much time with your loved ones as possible. When your body is healthy, you have more energy to plan fun activities or meals with friends and family. Whether you exercise, laugh, or just hang around, it helps you keep healthy, extending your time together. Large family gatherings are a superb opportunity to be grateful for the food you can taste, eat, and enjoy. Meanwhile, you're surrounded by loved ones - the best of both worlds. Meals foster a greater appreciation for your body's ability to intake nutrients, keeping you healthy.

You Can Enjoy the Weather - Any Weather

When you're healthy, the weather doesn't pose any issue for being outdoors. If you find a fun outside activity, you'll enjoy it. If you live in an area known for scorching summers, use the mornings for refreshing walks or sitting on your terrace. Small experiences like enjoying your morning beverage and breathing the fresh air might seem uneventful for many people. However, for those who can't do this due to poor health, doing it even once would mean everything. Whether you walk, sit, meditate, or do something else while observing the weather, be grateful for the experiences your body offers, the breathtaking sights, and the beautiful sounds. Can you dance in the rain freely, without pain? If yes, be grateful because many people would give everything for this experience. Even if you need help getting around, there are plenty of ways to enjoy the weather. The key is to concentrate on what you can achieve with your body rather than what you can't.

It Fosters Kindness

A healthy body leads to a healthy mind, and you feel your best when both are in sync. Have you ever felt so good you just wanted to share your well-being with someone in any way possible? Perhaps you were driven to random acts of kindness, like letting someone go in front of you in the grocery store line or spreading joy by greeting everyone with a big smile. When you feel good, those around you will notice it and inspire them to feel better, too. If you've ever been this happy, be grateful your health allowed it.

It Enables You to Play with Your Pets

If you have pets requiring a lot of activity, and you can join them while having fun, be grateful. Without good health, you wouldn't be able to spend as much time with them. Being able to create memories with your animal companions makes your time together all the more precious. Not to mention the benefits spending time with pets has on your physical and mental health. You don't have to be able to run with your dog to be active with them. If you can walk with them using a wheelchair, appreciate it. It's better than not doing it at all.

You Have a Sound Mental Health

The thought of sound mental health is often pushed to the background when people talk about appreciating their health. However, showing gratitude for your mental health improves your psychological state. It helps you clear your mind when stressed and cope with the symptoms of different conditions. A sound mind is fundamental for meaningful conversations and contributes to building healthy relationships. Even in tough times when you want to give up, your body and mind will always be there to support you. If you have ever felt you couldn't possibly get over the grief of losing a loved one, and yet you did, be thankful to your mind for allowing it.

It Allows You to Do Everything You Enjoy

Have you ever felt tired after an endless day of walking, running errands, spending time with your children or grandchildren, cleaning, and doing chores around the house? It takes a lot of footsteps during the day to accomplish a daily routine. If your legs are powerful enough to carry you around, be grateful. If they cannot, then appreciate the rest of your body. For example, the core muscles allow you to sit upright and move in your chair or arms strong enough to lift and carry what you enjoy, like your pet, children, or grandchildren. Be thankful even if you can do as little as reaching for a cup on your nightstand.

For all those wonderful mums: Be grateful for the miracle your body created. Did it change your body? It most certainly did, but it's all the more reason to be grateful for your body's little imperfections. They're a testimony to your body's power.

You Can Be Fully Present

A healthy body and mind enable you to calm your wayward thoughts and the fight-or-flight response during stress. Moreover, they encourage you to learn to focus on being present to cope with similar situations in the future. Mindfulness exercises are a fantastic way to channel positive energy and thoughts. It's another enthralling ability of your body to be grateful for.

You Have a Beating Heart

Did you know that an average person's heart beats over 3 billion times during their life? That's a lot of work, yet it's often taken for granted. Your heart sustains your circulatory system, pumping blood to your organs and keeping you alive. It empowers your lungs to take in oxygen to create fuel for your body and heal it from oxidative stress. Your heart is a powerful machine, so ensure you appreciate it daily (even if it needs a little help working).

Remember to end your day with gratitude and keep smiling.

CHAPTER 8

Step 7 – Nature

This is the 7th step of creating your list of appreciating the goodness of life and learning to be happier. Currently, your list contains items about health, family, body, relationships, and lifestyle you're grateful and happy about. These items have made you realize there's much to be grateful for, and reliving these happy moments adds to your happiness and overall well-being. Creating a list of things you're grateful for is always fun. There are endless things about your life and humanity to be happy and grateful about. However, this chapter seeks to enlighten you on the role of nature in happiness and gratitude.

Some countless documented evidence and theories prove the role of nature in enhancing mood and happiness, citing instances of trees, flowers, insects, and a beautiful horizon contributing to positive feelings. Nature is a great way to relax and be happier.

Life without Nature

To fully understand how to be grateful for nature and its influence on your happiness and gratitude, you must ask, "Where would I be without nature?"

A world without the provisions of the natural ecosystem is difficult to imagine because you'll be looking at an imbalanced and drastically unsustainable world. Lives would be compromised by the absence of nature. Your physical health would suffer due to insufficient food and sunlight to keep the body warm. Basic needs won't be met as clean water, air, and food will be absent. Plants and trees are natural filters for the air you breathe. A world without them would cause catastrophic failures in your respiratory system. The lack of natural food sources will affect food production and prices. Humans would have to outsource materials for food which would be expensive.

Creativity and mental health would wane drastically. Nature is an avenue for inspiration, experience, creativity, and awe. A world without these provisions would be dull. A world without green spaces like gardens and forests and blue spaces like lakes and oceans would be without aesthetic appeal and relief. The absence of calm and connectedness nature would lead to decreased quality of life, increased stress, and mental health issues.

Different tragedies would emerge from a world without nature. There'd be a struggle for limited resources, and people lacking nature's calming effect; hence, depression, anxiety, and anger would be the prevalent emotion.

Humans would be less inspired. There'll be no species diversity and fewer opportunities for rejuvenation, relaxation, and introspection. A world without nature would deprive humans of essential growth, survival, and happiness benefits.

Reason to Be Grateful for Nature

There's much to be grateful for in nature, from the sun giving light to the earth's natural ecosystem, nature's provisions benefiting daily lives, the food system, and nature's influence in maintaining the earth's balance. Consider the following:

The Sun

The sun provides energy for the plants to blossom and effortlessly radiates over mountains and clouds to brighten your day. The sun's energy warms the planet, keeping you warm in cold seasons. The beauty of the sunrise is one of the universe's many wonders. Although sunlight might be intense at intervals, its presence is absolute in the world's ecosystem. The moon reflects the sun's rays and controls the tides.

The Ecosystem

The ecosystem provides plants adding aesthetic value to the environment, and is a food source. Plants use sunlight and rain for their growth. The clouds provide water in the rain, later recycled through evaporation. Water in the environment forms rivers, lakes, and oceans, the habitat for aquatic animals. Water serves as transportation, irrigation, and resource for towns and municipalities. The snow that falls on mountains provides skiing opportunities and fun to play in; the little insects are crucial in the ecosystem, especially pollination, which produces beautiful flowers, and the animals helping maintain the natural balance are all part of the natural things people should be thankful for.

Nature provides many reasons to be grateful, starting with its power to awaken your mind and senses to new possibilities and responsibilities. Tapping into the beauty of nature, you reach creative heights and can discover new flows fueling your thinking and productivity. Nature has a relaxing effect on the mind. The sound of a river, a passing wind, and leaves brushing on each other can create a calming effect. Nature helps you relax and feel rejuvenated and alert. It teaches resilience and adaptation by studying the activities of other actors in the environment.

Nature serves an immense purpose to man, and usually, people overlook its importance. Without nature, mankind would be nowhere. Humans would be non-existent since the existence of mankind depends on it. Nature supplies the earth with the necessities for existence. It replenishes itself and can be depended upon by future generations. Being grateful for nature should be regularly practiced in your journey to become happier and more grateful. During your daily walks, reflect on how nature influences your routine, and you'll be amazed at how much you benefit from it. It'll provide you with enough information to make your list.

How Does Nature Improve Happiness

Nature is important in maintaining physical, emotional, and psychological health. Spending time in a natural environment helps you live more creative, healthier, and happier lives. Some of the proven ways nature adds to your happiness include:

- **It Makes You Feel Alive**

Being outdoors encourages a feeling of being alert and alive. It fills you with a burst of energy. Nature provides an opportunity for physical exercise and to move outside your homes and offices. It helps you escape work stress and your daily routine. Being in nature makes you feel vitalized and eager to explore the outdoors to your satisfaction. With its numerous sights and sounds, an awakening of the mind and body boosts an individual's happiness.

- **Nature Decreases Stress**

Stress is a limiting factor to people's happiness. Increased stress leads to anger and distress in persons. Nature helps reduce stress. Being in a natural setting, looking outdoors through a window, and listening to the sound of a flowing river and the rustling leaves by the wind reduce stress. Although physical exercises like hiking help, nature augments it. Nature helps you relax, reduces anxiety, and strengthens focus. A relaxed mind isn't bothered by upsetting thoughts, promoting happier living. As your stress is eliminated, you become lighter at heart and more rejuvenated.

- **It Boosts Creativity**

Nature is filled with aesthetic appeal and can help you find new ways to be creative. Nature helps clear the mind of thoughts clouding your thinking and creativity, opening ways for inspiration. Fatigue and stress cloud creativity, and nature feels like a breath of fresh air and a window into new creative wells. The mind is free and open to new ideas in a setting allowing peaceful thinking; it is less frustrated and restrained and facilitates creating fresh ideas.

- **Nature Boosts Physical and Mental Health**

In addition to its many benefits, nature adds to your happiness by boosting your mental and physical health. Spending time in the natural environment helps reduce depression, anxiety, and stress. It refreshes your mind and body, leading to a happier life. It improves moods, boosts creativity, and generates positivity. Apart from promoting physical activities, nature is an opportunity for bonding and connecting with others. Whether during group physical activities or natural outings, nature allows for social bonding and interaction, creating memories and experiences fostering happiness.

In your approach to becoming happier and more grateful, realizing the role of nature in your life gives you something to be grateful for. A world without nature would be difficult to fathom as your mind couldn't imagine the countless shortcomings that would arise.

By being grateful for nature, there's a myriad of benefits you can reflect on and be thankful for. You live every day on the provisions of nature, so you should be thankful for its support for humans. The sun gives light and energy; it warms the planets and supports plant growth. Plants help filter the air, provide food, and are natural resources to produce various required products. The water cycle supporting plants, humans, and aquatic life are from nature. The rain, the animals and insects, the trees, and the rivers provide many benefits that only make you wonder in awe and end your day in gratitude. Reflecting on these aspects are the reasons to be grateful for nature.

Nature offers serenity and solace; its beauty, captivating landscapes, and amazing phenomena awaken people's wonder and gratitude. The awe-inspiring moments of nature fill people with wonder, excitement, and humility. It boosts creativity and enhances inspiration. It teaches about adaptability, resilience, and interdependence. The different parts of nature depend on each other; it's a constant reminder to open up to the people and things around you to be happier.

Nature benefits mental health by helping reduce stress and promoting overall happiness. A walk in the park, the thrills of an outdoor adventure, and the joy derived from bonding with others in a natural setting or during physical activities are ways nature replenishes energy.

Recognizing and Enjoying Nature

Nature promotes physical, mental, and emotional health, adding to a healthier and happier life. Being grateful for nature is a huge step toward happiness, but firstly, you must be acquainted with nature. You must see and experience the beauty of nature before you can appreciate it.

Recognizing and enjoying nature means visiting your immediate or local environment. Experiencing and learning about nature are fun activities. The following are information and activities to help you know and enjoy nature more:

- **Exploring and Wandering**

Nature is vast, and to enjoy it, you must step out of the comfort of your home. There's enough landscape out there for you to see and satisfy your curiosity. If it's your first time to enjoy and experience nature, exploring and wandering is a good place to start. You can bring a map, pen, and a camera to record the experience, but you will need curiosity and an accessible landscape.

- **Nature Art**

If you're creative or artistic, the outdoors would be fun. You can appreciate nature through art. Whether you can draw or not is irrelevant. Your ability to appreciate the beauty of the natural world around you and feel a deep connection to nature is relevant. Art is a great way to connect with nature, and no matter what you draw, it helps you see more to nature than what meets the eye.

- **Planting a Garden**

Gardening is a life-enhancing and interactive way to explore nature. Through gardening, you can feel responsible for your immediate surroundings and learn nature's cogent lessons while fostering a relationship with the natural environment. You'll learn about the earth's ecosystem, how plants grow, and the importance of insects. Gardening allows you to learn about nature while gaining a sense of responsibility.

- **Visiting Different Landscapes**

One of the easiest ways to learn about the patterns and varieties in nature is by visiting areas with different landscapes. People typically don't realize they're confined to one landscape. Nature is filled with different ecological communities, replete with diverse organisms that would fill you with wonder. Fields, forests, and climes house these ecosystems; you only have to take a walk or visit them.

The different ways nature sustains are more reasons to be thankful. Earth's biodiversity, diverse natural terrain, and the support it renders daily activities are tangible ways nature supports life. Appreciating nature helps cultivate deeper responsibility and gratitude toward the environment. Gratitude toward nature doesn't only entail appreciating its roles and benefits. It involves efforts to maintain the natural environment. Being grateful for nature opens people's minds and hearts, exposing them to countless ways to enrich lives and live in harmony with the world.

Nature encompasses everyone, and your interaction with it grows by the day. In your daily interaction with nature, be introspective and carefully observe how nature fills you with wonder and joy. Be grateful for nature, whether at work, school, or leisure. Gratitude for nature helps you feel relaxed, pleased, and refreshed, enhancing moods and happiness. When you seek to appreciate nature, you end your day with happiness.

Remember to end your day with gratitude and keep smiling.

CHAPTER 9

Step 8 - Gratitude for Things

Gratitude, no matter how cliché it sounds, is for a reason. Being blind to the things around you and losing sight of the small blessings makes something as simple as gratitude difficult. The truth is you already have so much to be grateful for; you've merely lost sight of it. If you continuously feel stuck in a rut, you can bet it stems from a lack of appreciation for the little things around you. Trudging through your day waiting for something new or exciting to happen to spark joy and add color to your day rarely happens. Why tie your joy to such unexpected sources? You should focus on what you have and what surrounds you and be sincerely grateful for them.

Practicing gratitude is one of the easiest ways to improve your outlook and find meaning and purpose. Consciously engaging in it daily and taking a few minutes in the day to actively give thanks for what you have can transform your life. Consider the following ways to imbibe gratitude:

Practicing Mindful Appreciation

In today's society, getting distracted by technological and physical devices is easy. TV, radio, billboards, posters, and social media messages urge people to desire more. These platforms constantly feed your eyes and ears with promotions of the latest products and lifestyles, increasing your desire for more. As a result, the desire always leads to wanting what you do not have, which is the grassroots for envy and discontent. However, by practicing gratitude for what you already possess, you can find greater happiness and satisfaction in life.

To live a life of gratitude, you must slow down and open your eyes to the simple blessings around you each day. Make it a habit to stop several times throughout the day to look around and truly appreciate what you have - especially the things you use every day. There's gratitude to be felt in all the little details around you, from the furniture in your home to the clothes you wear, that favorite shirt, dress, or jeans. Each item you possess serves a purpose and contributes to your daily life. They might not be the most extravagant or luxurious, but they are yours and significantly support and enrich your existence.

Notice the little details in your home, like the knick-knacks on your shelves, the pillows on your couch, and the rug under your feet. Appreciate how they make your space cozy and reflect your style. Pay attention to the tools and technology you rely on, like your TV or music speaker. Be grateful you have access to things that make your life easier and more enjoyable.

Find gratitude for the necessities you often take for granted, such as running water, electricity, shelter, transportation, and access to healthcare. Millions of people don't have these basic comforts, so be thankful you can afford them.

If you notice you are about to fall into ingratitude, catch yourself. Stop and correct your thinking when you are comparing your belongings to those of others. Rather than focusing on the many things you lack, focus on the abundance you already have around you. You need to continuously remind yourself that your happiness or joy is not defined by the possessions you do or do not own. By shifting your perspective on what matters, you can reframe and repurpose your thoughts to embrace gratitude for the things that have been and are serving you.

Incorporating gratitude for things into your daily practice has a way of enhancing your overall well-being. When you recognize and appreciate the objects contributing to your life, you can break free from the never-ending cycle of desire and find contentment in the present. Your possessions are not the source of your happiness, but when you cultivate gratitude for them, you can experience deeper joy and fulfillment.

Savor the Moment

Learn to live in the moment. The best way to practice gratitude is to slow down and savor the moment. Your busy life often doesn't allow you the time to appreciate the simple pleasures in each day. Making a conscious effort to live in the present and embrace the tiny details can greatly impact your gratitude and well-being. Pausing at intervals to take a moment to appreciate the objects contributing to your comfort, convenience, and enjoyment will help you acknowledge their value in your life, whether a cozy warm blanket, a reliable vehicle, a cherished book, a mug, or a kitchen appliance.

As you start your day, mindfully do the activities involving these items. Whether eating a meal, walking, cycling, or watching a movie with a loved one, focus on the experience. Say, "I'm grateful for my favorite bowl or that I can eat my favorite cereals," or "I am thankful for my sneakers or running shoes and my bike, which is still usable," or "I am grateful for my TV and sound system, and the power supply to power these appliances." Notice tastes, sounds, and sensations, appreciate each bite or step, and make eye contact.

Engage your senses in gratitude. It will deepen your connection with your belongings. As you use them, revel in the sight, touch, smell, sound, and taste of these items. Feel the fabric's texture against your skin, revel in the aroma of your favorite tea, listen to the soothing sound of your favorite music, and enjoy the taste of a nourishing meal. By fully immersing yourself in the experience of using or enjoying your possessions, you deepen your appreciation for them and cultivate profound gratitude. The key ingredient is "savor." Take in as much of the experience as possible; this will elevate your spirit, helping you stay thankful.

Express gratitude for simple pleasures - an umbrella for the sun or pouring rain, a fan or air conditioner for a cool breeze on a hot day, or a room heater on a cold night. Verbalize your appreciation for these little comforts. Say it out loud or write it down in a journal.

Furthermore, avoid comparing your belongings to those of others. Remember, everyone's journey is unique, and their possessions do not diminish your value. Instead, celebrate the achievements and acquisitions of others, and be genuinely happy for them. By practicing this mindset, envy gives way to admiration and gratitude.

Limiting distractions will do you much good by minimizing interruptions from societal messages and avoiding multitasking. Spend a few minutes each day unplugged from the chaos around you, and appreciate and savor the things around you, doing what you love.

Reflect on your day. At night before bed, think about your day and the moments you're grateful for. This simple practice helps reframe your mindset to be more positive and appreciative. You'll sleep better and wake up feeling more grateful.

Make it a habit to express gratitude for the little pleasures each day. Your outlook will change dramatically.

Keep a Gratitude Journal

As you note these personal belongings around you, write them down. Add it to the list you have successfully created over the past few days. Be intentional about it, as writing things down does wonders. You will be surprised how much further your list will grow with the little things surrounding you. Keeping a journal is one of the simplest ways to practice gratitude. All you need is a notebook or journal and a pen. Set aside a few minutes each day, like before bedtime or early in the morning, or you could even do it as you go about your day, jotting down a few things you're grateful for.

You could use other electronic options if moving around with a book is too much hassle. You can convert your phone's notepad to a journal or download an electronic journal. These will make it easier to write down what you are grateful for so you do not forget them. Focus on the simple pleasures and let your gratitude flow onto the page. Don't overthink it. Write what comes to mind.

Keeping a daily gratitude journal helps train your brain to notice the positives in your life. The more you do it, the more natural it will feel. You'll see your day through a gratitude lens without even trying. When life feels extra stressful or overwhelming, reading over your journal entries will remind you of how much you have to be grateful for.

Gratitude journals don't have to be lengthy. Jotting down three to five things a day, a few sentences for each can significantly affect your well-being and happiness.

Count Your Blessings for More Blessings

Your gratitude for the things around you is also recognizing that your possessions can be upgraded or replaced. This realization is great because it keeps you feeling content in the present while allowing you to maintain hope for the future. The point of gratitude is not to aspire for more. However, the desire for change and better improvement is natural. Wanting better is a normal part of a people's makeup. You shouldn't feel bad if you desire other things. The problem is making that desire take the front seat over everything else. There must be a balance between your aspirations and gratitude for what you already possess.

Stay grateful even as you strive for more. As you appreciate and are thankful for your belongings, you create a positive foundation to build your future.

Also, besides your long-term aspirations and desire, a short-term blessing to be grateful for is sound sleep and good health. At the end of the day, before retiring to bed, you conclude with a moment of gratitude for what accompanied you throughout the day and helped you make your day seamless. You reflect on the moments of joy, comfort, and convenience your possessions provided. This reflection can trigger fond memories of loved ones, places, occasions, and experiences, causing your worries to melt away. By expressing sincere gratitude for these items' positive impact on your life, you end your day feeling grateful and cultivate fulfillment and contentment, paving the way for a restful and rejuvenating sleep.

Move your attention away from the things you lack and focus on the countless things you own and benefit from. Appreciate their presence in your life and how they contribute to your daily experiences. As you do, let a smile spread across your face, knowing that these possessions, no matter how big or small, contribute to your well-being and bring you convenience, comfort, or pleasure. Embrace a mindset of abundance and appreciation, recognizing that what you have is enough.

Choosing gratitude helps you focus on life's blessings rather than shortcomings, which is the secret to finding daily contentment and joy. Make time each day to appreciate the little things around you and notice how it shifts your mindset and mood. Start small but be consistent. Keep a journal, share with others, and reflect on your day. The more you practice, the more natural gratitude will become. Before you know it, you'll be walking around with a smile and a heart full of thankfulness for this beautiful life you've been given. Remember, possessions are not meant to define your worth or happiness. They are tools serving a purpose, enhancing your life, or providing comfort. Embrace the understanding that your possessions do not determine your value. The newest gadgets, trendiest clothes, or grandest possessions do not guarantee lasting happiness. True contentment comes from within, from appreciating your life's simple joys and treasures.

Give it a shot - you have nothing to lose and everything to gain. The world always seems a little brighter when looking at it through the gratitude lens.

Remember to end your day with gratitude and keep smiling.

CHAPTER 10

Step 9 - Work

Children love role-playing games and dressing up as doctors, cops, firefighters, etc. These games allow them to act out what they want to be when they grow up, often dreaming big. Although it is still too early for them to think about a career, they find the idea of having a job and being independent fascinating. As a child, you probably watched your parents with awe and admiration as they woke up every morning purposefully to make their dreams come true. You probably couldn't wait for the day you become an employee.

However, as children grow into mature adults, they forget their fascination and excitement for having a job. Going to work every day becomes a tedious routine. Most people treat their job as a means to make money and earn a living. If they had a choice, they would probably never work again but live their life doing what they enjoy.

You spend most of your time complaining about your tyrant boss, the long commute, or your competitive, unpleasant co-workers. You are no longer that little child who couldn't wait to make a difference in the world. You forget that your job allows you to achieve goals and pays your bills.

If you spend time with your unemployed friends or family members, you will realize how good you have it. Their life is unstable, and they don't know if they can pay their bills every month or support their family. Many have lost their sense of purpose and ambition. It makes your issues with your horrible boss or nosy co-worker insignificant. Doesn't it?

Consider yourself lucky if you do something you love. Many people are stuck in dead-end careers and only work for the money. They've lost their spark and passion, and nothing in their jobs excites them anymore. So, if you don't get along with your boss or co-workers, you should still be grateful for having your dream job. However, if you aren't enthusiastic about your career, maybe you have a supportive boss or friendly co-workers who make your life easier.

Whatever the circumstances, be grateful for the financial security and a reason to get out of bed every morning.

Today, pause at every chance to contemplate your job and express your gratitude for your work.

The Importance of Having a Job

Your job isn't just a source of income. It gives a sense of identity. When people get to know you, the first thing they ask after your name is, "What do you do?" The meaning behind this question isn't only what you do for money or your job; they want to know what you are doing with your life. When you say I am a teacher, doctor, architect, engineer, accountant, etc., you are saying who you are, not only what you do.

Whether you know of it or not, you associate your sense of self with your profession. Your career has become a part of your identity. It isn't your whole identity but a large part of it since you spend most of your life in your job, and it can impact every aspect of your life. If you calculate how many hours you spend at your office daily, you will realize you spend most of your time working.

Your job gives you purpose, responsibility, and direction. You feel that you matter and are making a difference in the world. When you work toward your goals, you can be an inspiration to your family and friends. You feel confident, capable, and accomplished. For instance, when you go out and meet new people, you will feel good about yourself when talking about your job rather than saying, "I am unemployed."

You can learn new skills on the job. Many companies provide training courses for their employees to advance in their careers. These skills stimulate your brain so you can be engaged and alert at work. You learn what it means to be a part of a team, connect with like-minded people, and make friendships that could last a lifetime.

One of the best perks of having a job is financial security. Getting a steady paycheck provides stability and allows you to support yourself and your family, making life easier and more comfortable. Also, you become independent and self-sufficient. You feel proud because you can afford everything you want rather than getting into debt to travel or buy something.

Having a job reduces stress, boosts your confidence, increases your energy, promotes better sleep, improves your mood, and impacts every aspect of your mental and physical health.

Do you remember what life was like during COVID-19? You were cooped up at home for months and couldn't go to work or leave the house. Although most people enjoy spending time at home with their families, you need some distance from them to get out of the house and meet new people. Waking up early every morning can be exhausting and a chore, but many people realized the value of having a routine and an active lifestyle during the pandemic.

However, you probably don't notice that your job is a blessing. You take it for granted or treat it as a chore. You might hate waking up early in the morning, huffing and puffing whenever your boss asks you to work overtime, and can't stand some of your co-workers. If you pause for a moment and think of what your job represents and how it impacts every aspect of your life, you will be grateful every day for this gift.

Why You Should Be Grateful
for Your Job

Nothing is perfect. If you dissect every area of your life, you will find something to complain about. However, practicing gratitude changes your perspective, and you will focus on the positives, making the negatives seem small or trivial in comparison. Moreover, you become a happier, better, and more engaged employee, increasing your productivity. Ultimately, gratitude can improve your professional life, making you successful in your career.

Many people believe the grass is greener on the other side, such as, "My life would be better if I get promoted or a raise," or "I would be happier if I could get a job in another company." They postpone their happiness and gratitude until their circumstances change. However, the future is never guaranteed, and you can never know if another job or promotion will improve your situation. All you have is the here and now, so you should cherish this present moment. Even if you manage to get a raise or achieve one of your dreams, you won't be happy if you aren't practicing gratitude. You will always be waiting for the next big thing.

By practicing gratitude, you appreciate everything about your job - the easy commute, having a nice lunch with your co-workers, your boss's encouragement, or a promotion. Since you spend most of your adult life working, make the best of it. Be grateful for your job and work hard to make something of yourself.

Naturally, you will have bad days, like when another employee takes credit for your work, or your boss yells at you in front of your co-workers. These situations can make it hard to be grateful. Remember, everyone has bad days, but this doesn't change the fact that you are lucky to have a job, healthcare, and can pay rent.

How to Be Grateful for Your Job

You must change your mindset and be grateful for your work to be truly happy. Think about that paycheck you receive every month that allows you to put food on the table, clothes on your back, and fuel in the car. You could put a small amount aside for emergencies, spoil yourself and your family with an expensive dinner, or go on a holiday. Remember, many people live in poverty with barely enough money to buy the necessities. They might have to skip meals, live without heating, and wear hand-me-downs.

The next time your boss is unkind to you, take a deep breath before you get angry and think, "I am very grateful for my job. It gives me something to do and earns me money." Remind yourself of everything you've gained because of your job, like making close friends, good health benefits, or maybe you get to work outdoors and enjoy the beautiful weather. Perhaps you work in health or a school and help people every day. So, the next time ungratefulness creeps into your mind, look for a few things you can be grateful about your job and repeat them to yourself. If you think hard enough, it's guaranteed you will find at least three.

Avoid negative words when thinking or talking about your job. Rather than saying, "I hate waking up in the morning," say, "Although waking up in the morning isn't always easy, it is refreshing and beneficial for my mind and body." Always use positive statements and steer clear of words like hate.

By changing your thought pattern from hating your job to being grateful, you will feel happier and more satisfied about your job.

Practice gratitude for having a job by repeating these statements:

- I am grateful for having a job
- I am thankful for the sense of purpose, direction, and identity my job gives me
- I am happy to learn new skills helping me advance in my career
- I am grateful for a steady paycheck and the ability to afford the things I want
- I am grateful for the stability and security my job gives me
- Thank you, boss, for being supportive and believing in me
- Thank you to my co-workers who made me feel I am a part of the team
- I am grateful for my mistakes at work because they give me learning opportunities
- I am thankful for the easy commute
- I am happy to share lunch with my co-workers and catch up in the middle of our busy day

- I am grateful for not worrying every month about paying my rent or bills
- I am thankful my job made me a stronger and more resilient person
- I am grateful for the sense of accomplishment I get every day from my job
- I am grateful for making a difference in the world
- I am thankful for the intellectual stimulation I get from my job
- I am grateful I have something to do every day rather than doing nothing at home
- Thank you to my competitive co-workers. You push me to work hard and be a better employee
- I am happy to be recognized for the work I do
- It warms my heart that I can help people through my job
- I am thankful for the delicious cup of coffee I drink at work every morning
- I am grateful for my nice office
- I am thankful for the benefits my job gives me
- I am happy to have insurance and healthcare
- I am proud to support myself and my family
- I am grateful for the connections I made through my job
- I am always happy to help my co-workers
- I am thankful for not having money concerns
- I am grateful for the fascinating stories I get to tell about my job

- I am grateful to tell the world I am a doctor, architect, teacher, accountant, writer, etc.
- I am always pleased to see the joy and satisfaction on my customers' faces
- I am grateful for landing this job and working hard to create the life I have always wanted

Your job is a blessing. Many people dream of being in your place. So, be grateful for your work today and every day. You will appreciate it more.

Remember to end your day with gratitude and keep smiling.

CHAPTER 11

Step 10 – Take a Break

Do you ever feel you're working on autopilot, going through the motions, and not being fully present at the moment? Have you ever questioned the purpose behind your actions or wondered if there was more to life than this seemingly robotic life? Well, you're not alone. Nowadays, most people have no time to spare and spend every waking second trying to complete tasks, finish chores, or meet deadlines. Even when doing something you enjoy, it seems like something that must be done instead of something you want to do. You're constantly bombarded with responsibilities, pressures, and unrealistic expectations.

This modern world has made life a competition over who's the most productive or who has the most achievements. However, everyone fails to realize that life is not all about work. What good would financial security bring if you don't have your family to share it with? Or why does having a spotless house matter more than spending time with your kids? The hustle culture so glorified today is nothing but a never-ending spinning of your wheels. When you push yourself over your limits, you're likely to become exhausted. Initially, it will seem like everything is working out and you can be superhuman. However, you'll start to get overwhelmed, and your brain will simply give up after a while. Is that how you want to live your life?

Although these habits are common among overachievers, they do more harm than good. You're likely to burn out when you try to be everything to everyone and do everything all at once. There's only so much your body, mind, and soul can take. You might often wish for a time-freeze option you could get for life, just so you can take a breath, relax, and exist without doing anything. There are no time-freeze options in real life, but you can take a break. Take a break from your hectic work, the never-ending chores that pile up every day, the constant academic expectations of your parents, or just to take a breather.

It's true not everyone has the luxury to get up and go on vacation. You have jobs, a home, kids to care for, and deadlines to meet. These are understandable reasons. However, taking a break does not take more than 5 minutes if that's all you can afford. Just five minutes of your day, and you'll stop feeling like a cog in the machine, grinding against the other cogs, trying to make the system work. You owe this little to yourself, and no one else will do it for you. Taking time for yourself doesn't mean you don't value your job, are not serious about your studies, or don't love your kids enough. Everyone needs space from time to time; without it, you will go crazy.

It's perfectly okay to want a break occasionally. Not only is it okay, but it should also be encouraged to help fight against the stress constantly wearing you down. Moreover, taking a break, mindfully and present, will help you see this life for what it is; a blessing. You'll realize how beautiful this world is and how many great things you have. You'll feel content, fulfilled, and happy with your lifestyle. Scientific explanations have proven why taking frequent breaks is essential for your health.

Why Taking Breaks Is Essential

Just as getting enough sleep is essential for your brain to function properly, rest is equally important to promote brain function. When you let your brain rest, the same consolidation processes take place as when you sleep. By allowing yourself downtime with minimum distractions in your surroundings, you improve your brain's capacity to focus and be attentive and creative. Merely five minutes of rest can make you feel fresh and allows you to process new information and tie it to other concepts.

You can take two approaches to rest your brain. You can slow down and rest or be active, like going for a walk. The main purpose of a break is to help you relax and feel refreshed afterward. For instance, many think taking a break means scrolling on their phones or watching another episode. However, this makes them more tired. Firstly, excessive screen time is not healthy. When you use your breaks to look at screens, it's no different than when you're working. Your brain should get a boost from rest, not become more tired, which happens when you look at a screen.

Secondly, a good break would mean you were in your resting brain state. What's that, you wonder? Your brain can be in several states. When the brain is actively working, it produces beta waves, while when it's resting, alpha waves are produced. Sleeping produces delta waves, and while daydreaming, your brain produces theta waves. To keep your brain healthy and active, spending time in different brain states is crucial. When you spend all your time working, worrying about one thing or another, you only stay in your active state, ultimately making your brain sluggish or ineffective.

For example, have you ever experienced where you couldn't remember someone's name or a fact, but it popped into your mind later when you were resting? Or, maybe, a problem or issue that seemed impossible to solve was later very simple? When this happens, your brain goes from its active to resting stage. It's still working, but even better than when you're stressed about the issue, even if you're not consciously aware. As a result, your problem is solved easily. This is the power a good break can have on your mind.

The best part about taking breaks is there's no specific duration to adhere to when resting your mind. The most challenging part is allowing yourself to take a break, not forcing yourself through the motions diverting your mind elsewhere. Take short breaks throughout the day to feel active and fresh; it will help you be grateful for everything in life.

How to Take Beneficial Breaks

It will, of course, take time to explore which activities you enjoy during your breaks. Everyone is different. For some, listening to music while drinking a cup of coffee is refreshingly the same as practicing yoga or meditation for others. Moreover, how frequently you take breaks depends on your situation. For instance, if you have to juggle a job, household tasks, and kids, it's certainly not feasible to take a five-minute break every hour. On the other hand, if you only have to deal with work or simple studies, taking a five-minute break every hour can prove quite effective and might even help you handle your procrastination habits. Consider the following aspects when deciding how to take breaks:

1. Calm Your Central Nervous System

If you want your breaks to be restful, they cannot include chores. For instance, doing laundry or running an errand counts as a break from your job, but it does not give the benefits of proper rest. You wouldn't say, "I took a break to do laundry." If you want your break to refresh and energize you, spend time calming your central nervous system. When you're at work, doing a chore, studying for a test, or doing any of the thousands of tasks you have during the day, your nervous system has you in a fight or flight mode. If you're constantly in this state, you could develop mental or physical issues like chronic stress, anxiety, fatigue, etc. It does not mean stress is intrinsically bad for your body. However, excessive stress can affect your nervous system, which has several negative side effects. When you choose something calming to do, like reading a book or spending time in nature, you allow your nervous system to return to its baseline state.

2. Shift from Doing to Being

As previously discussed, today's culture emphasizes productivity and focuses on a person's accomplishments more than anything else, making it difficult for anyone to slow down and relax. For instance, the first time you meet someone, they usually ask, "What do you do?" Society judges people by their success, the cause for everyone running on autopilot and burning out. Although it's not a bad thing to set goals and work toward them, it helps keep your life in check and gives you meaning. However, the idea that you must constantly do something leads to unhealthy coping mechanisms. Some people even feel guilty when they're not doing something productive with their time, and many struggle with imposter syndrome due to the fake niceties on social media.

You must first develop a mindset to show yourself love to cope. If you judge your worth by how much time you spend being productive, how do you think other people will judge you? Change the way you think, and learn to recognize when you're in over your head and need to take a break. When you take a break, turn off every distraction. Put your phone aside, and allow yourself to just exist in the moment. Get as little input as possible; this is a time for resting your brain and not giving it new information to process. Stop overthinking your problems. They'll be there to worry about after your break. At this moment, just relax, breathe in the fresh air, and look at the beautiful sky, grass, trees, mountains, and nice views. Do nothing more than exist.

3. Be Kind to Yourself

If your breaks aren't helping as much as you thought they would, don't fret. Don't try to maximize the health benefits of your breaks, and never berate yourself if it doesn't happen. Know that you don't have to do everything perfectly. If you can't make time for frequent breaks often, that's fine. If you use your breaks to get other work done, that's understandable, too. There's no need for self-criticism. However, keep in sync with your body, know when it's time to stop and rest, and when you can keep going. There's no point in beating yourself up. You're practicing gratitude and taking breaks for yourself, so if you're not kind to yourself during the process, then it is all for nothing.

A Few Ideas for Taking Breaks

If you're unsure what to do when taking a break, consider these ideas:

- Walk in the park or garden
- Sit down with a steaming cup of coffee
- Watch the clouds change shape
- Lie on the grass and just breathe
- Take your dog for a walk
- Go for a swim
- Walk along the beach

- Cuddle up with a book
- Lie in front of the fireplace
- Take your kids to the amusement park
- Look at the stars
- Stretch and do a quick exercise routine to get your blood flowing
- Take a power nap to recharge and refresh your mind
- Listen to your favorite music or a calming playlist
- Enjoy a quick mindfulness or breathing exercise
- Step outside and get some fresh air for a few minutes
- Do a crossword or Sudoku puzzle to stimulate your brain
- Have a healthy snack to boost your energy levels
- Spend a few minutes chatting with a coworker or friend
- Watch a funny or inspiring video to lift your mood
- Practice a mini meditation session to relax and clear your mind
- Engage in a creative activity like doodling or coloring
- Write down a gratitude list or affirmations to cultivate positivity
- Play a quick online game or solve a brain teaser
- Do a mini decluttering task to create order and calm
- Take a few minutes to plan and prioritize your upcoming tasks
- Watch a short TED Talk or informative video on a topic of interest
- Browse through inspirational quotes or read a motivational article

- Indulge in a few minutes of daydreaming or visualization
- Enjoy a cup of herbal tea or a refreshing glass of water

Throughout the day, you get many chances to live your life, actually live it, not just go through the motions. If you're not grabbing these opportunities by the throat, you're missing out on many beautiful experiences. So, enjoy these little joys life gives you, and you'll realize how beautiful this world is. Read that book, get wet in the rain, do yoga, go out to eat, have fun with your kids, try everything.

Remember to end your day with gratitude and keep smiling.

CHAPTER 12

Step 11 - Reflect and Say Thank You

In your journey through life, you will encounter people who will eventually form a circle around your life. These people become a significant part of your decision-making. They include your parents, siblings, relatives, friends, teachers, co-workers, business partners, doctors, and others who have contributed positively to your life. They define your interaction with the outside world and give meaning to your existence. Sometimes, you fail to realize the magnitude of their impact on you due to familiarity. Therefore, it's necessary to reflect on how big of an influence they have been on you.

Essentially, listing the things you are grateful for gives room for reflection and appreciation. What you might have thought insignificant suddenly becomes significant. You will realize that without the little efforts of others, you wouldn't be where you are today.

Why Reflect?

Being grateful is a choice. A grateful person observes the events of a situation and how they influence them and appreciate the peace and good it brings. Gratitude helps you experience positive emotions, build good relationships, and enjoy these experiences. It is like a vitamin for good health, and without reflecting on these past and present experiences, you won't recognize their impact and express gratitude. Hence, the importance of reflecting.

Reflecting gives room for expressing gratitude. It helps you recognize people's positive impact on your life. These experiences, however normal they seem, are worth being grateful for. Remember when you received assistance from a friend to settle a pressing need? You realize how important their presence was at that moment. Without them, you probably had a hard time figuring your way out. The same applies to your relationship with your parents and guardians. They were solely responsible for providing basic needs, settling school fees, and ensuring you were up and doing. It doesn't matter how little their contribution might have been; receiving their love is worth relishing because not many people have these seemingly little benefits.

You will feel happier and more cheerful as you acknowledge these experiences and benefits. Reflecting and journaling the moments when you feel grateful makes you more content and willing to express gratitude.

Reflecting strengthens your positive emotions. Instead of feeling overwhelmed or unappreciated by the activities surrounding you, ponder on simple pleasures like the feel of the sun's rays on a bright Monday morning, the short but enjoyable conversation you had with your friend while working in the office, and similar pleasurable experiences, can help you improve your focus toward a lifestyle of positivity.

Also, reflecting can help you avoid being self-centered. Contemplating past experiences of receiving help can naturally make you want to reciprocate in the future. It might not be necessary, but it will help you understand people's actions and strengthen your relationships.

Expressing Gratitude – Saying Thank You with Action

Saying a heartfelt 'thank you' is the simplest and most direct way of expressing gratitude to those who have impacted your life positively. However, there are other ways you can express your gratitude. For example, showing gratitude with gestures leaves a long-lasting impression of appreciation on people. Mixing your appreciative words with gestures speaks volumes of your gratitude. Try the following gestures:

- **Give a Gift**

People who receive gifts at events, such as birthday celebrations, weddings, and anniversaries, are usually excited because they recognize the thoughtfulness of those who present them. Also, you can give a gift to someone who has positively impacted your life to show how grateful you are to have them in your life. A thoughtful gift has the special effect of strengthening the bond of a relationship, especially if it can be kept and treasured for a long time.

- **Pay a Visit**

Many have long-distance relationships with family, friends, and business partners. Although there is constant communication between both parties through video and voice calls, squeezing time from your busy schedule or embarking on a vacation to visit them in person is a big show of gratitude for their presence in your life.

- **Openly Show Appreciation**

Walking up to a person to tell them how much of an impact they have had on you and recounting the experiences when they turned up for you is another way of expressing gratitude. Showing appreciation encourages people to uphold their values since you represent their impact. You could do a shout-out or post about them on your Instagram or Facebook story; this is a more profound way of proclaiming your gratitude.

- **Write a Handwritten Letter**

In today's world, people mostly resolve to online texting rather than in the early periods of handwritten letters and mailing. You can show gratitude by writing a handwritten letter. Handwritten letters are almost extinct, which makes them more cherished and valued. It would be perceived as very thoughtful when writing letters to show gratitude. It's a more meaningful way of saying, "You are worth my time."

- **Make a Family Toast**

You are well acquainted with your family members first before associating with strangers who eventually become friends. They are bonded to you forever by blood, and their presence abounds with wholeness.

It's somehow easy to not consciously regard the little things families do for love –the support they provide by their presence, the comfort they give in trying times, and many other thoughtful gestures which sometimes seem like an entitlement. Suppose you point out these seemingly little gestures. You will realize they constitute a greater reason why you are emotionally stable today. You can show your gratitude by setting up an impromptu family dinner and making a toast to their support and show of love in the past.

Benefits of Reflecting Gratitude

Several mental and physical benefits are gained from practicing gratitude. If you commit yourself to appreciation, you can benefit in various ways:

- Reflecting gratitude toward people can help you focus more on your daily activities. It reduces stress at work or when attending to a difficult situation. If you practice reflecting gratitude, you will see challenges as opportunities and fuel your emotional resilience.

- A benefit of reflecting gratitude not usually discussed is it improves sleep. You will experience less disturbance and more comfort sleeping because your gratitude will stir up satisfaction. It clouds your mind with positive thoughts about yourself and others and repels negativity.

- Many studies have shown that reflecting gratitude helps you master self-control and boosts self-esteem. Approaching the world around you with gratitude refines how you perceive your worth. Due to your perceived value, people around you are willing to invest their time, energy, and resources in you. These gestures internalize that you are an important personality in the life of those around you.

- Reflecting on gratitude can improve how you relate to people. By expressing appreciation to your friends and family, you give them the notion you care for them. It opens the door to better relationships.

For instance, informing your friends of how you appreciate them turning up for you regularly makes them recognize their value in your life. They will continue showing up when you need them.

- Other than the social and mental benefits of reflecting gratitude, health benefits are associated with this practice. For instance, you will notice that as you reflect gratitude toward your loved ones, the tension and rise in blood pressure will subsidize. It can be the medicine for your cardiovascular health.

If you regularly practice reflecting gratitude, you will likely exhibit healthy behaviors like sticking to a healthy diet or exercising regularly. It is usually a result of not viewing healthy lifestyle decisions as obstacles but as opportunities.

Cultivating Gratitude through Reflection

Learning to grow your gratitude continually requires watering the reflection process through commitment.

- **Be Mindful**

Learning not to rush things and taking time to relish your humble beginnings is a way of cultivating gratitude. As you reflect on how time and people have helped you grow, your mind will linger on the pleasant experiences and pull you out of worry and rumination.

Direct your mind to the experiences and relationships you appreciate daily. For instance, you could savor the smell of freshly baked bread as you walk to the bakery close to your workplace. Being mindful of these little things can foster gratitude.

Another good practice is setting time to listen to audiobooks that help you meditate and reflect. It instills calmness, incorporating gratitude and mindfulness.

- **Use a Journal**

Several things should be considered before keeping a gratitude journal. First, decide if you want a physical journal or a digital device like a phone or computer where you will make your notes. Second, decide when the journal should be updated. It could be done at the end of every week by taking time during the weekend to write down four or five experiences you appreciated during the week.

Many people make it a habit to write down what they are grateful for before bed. This can benefit you. As much as this practice can be exciting and greatly anticipated, don't write so often that it becomes a chore. Also, stay consistent with the time you initially set to make your notes.

You can write about the new friends you made, events you attended, and other general experiences. Also, write about those unexpected experiences, like a short chat with a friendly stranger, the relaxing massage you received from your partner after a long working day, and many other experiences that might not seem so significant. Ensure the write-up is detailed, even if it is short. For example, you could include the details the stranger made that got you smiling.

- **Learn the Lessons**

It's common for people to regret past experiences. It could be when they lost a loved one, failed an important exam, had a financial crisis, or missed out on an opportunity to date their dream person. Everyone has relatable experiences that disappointed, ashamed, and left them heartbroken. However, another side to view these events is the lessons learned from these experiences.

Asking questions like, "How did these events contribute to my growth?" "What behavior did they cause me to adopt?" Reflective questions can help you find lessons to keep you moving forward. It will spur gratitude, and you will journal your review for future reflection.

As much as practicing gratitude can be a mood booster, it takes considerable time before its impact reflects on your mental health and well-being. You must exercise patience practicing gratitude. As you continually engage in these exercises, your relationships improve, and your stress is relieved.

Reflecting will make you think about your actions and how people treat you. Without learning to reflect, you might have the wrong conclusions. Today, reflect on four persons who have largely impacted your life and write down why you should thank them. You might be inspired to write them a letter of appreciation or relish their thoughts.

Remember to end your day with gratitude and keep smiling.

CHAPTER 13

Step 12 – Strangers in the Street

In pursuing gratitude, you can explore various areas and aspects of your life worthy of appreciation and gratitude. You recognize the importance of gratitude in aspects like your work, possessions, relationships, people, family, nature, health, and many more blessings surrounding you. As you approach the end of this amazing journey, there is more to extend your gratitude toward. A gratitude for the strangers you meet daily. Learning to extend your gratitude beyond the people you know and are close to is important - to the strangers or those you hardly know who significantly influence your great day.

By acknowledging the persons who impact your daily life substantially beyond your regular activities, you send positive energy that will come back to you in more ways throughout your day. An ancient spiritual saying is, "Whatever you give to someone beside you with your whole heart never goes away but returns a hundredfold." Gratitude is a form of giving. As you offer appreciation to the person wholeheartedly, it draws the universe's energy to favor you.

Your gratitude isn't for what you stand to get; that would be ill-intent and considered selfish. Rather, it is truly appreciating the great effort these individuals put into their work to help you have a seamless day. So, buckle up as you get set for another gratitude ride.

Several People to Be Grateful For

In today's modern-day hustle and bustle, it is possible to overlook the individuals who quietly work and perform their duties to make your life better, safer, and more convenient. These persons are important in society but often go unnoticed. Several times a day, you will be in contact with many people. However, the mediums of contact and result are always the same, whether on the phone, via email, or face-to-face; the result is you get something from them. It's the people in the stores and restaurants you frequent, on the train or bus, at your favorite cafe, at your kid's school, and in your workplace. The options are nearly inexhaustible. These individuals deserve your gratitude because their presence has relieved you of stress, even if it's by a single percent.

Cast your mind on the individuals you encounter regularly who provide you with a service:

- The individuals on standby to stock the supermarket shelves to ensure you have the necessary products

- The garbage collectors in your neighborhood diligently dispose of your trash, maintaining cleanliness and hygiene on your behalf within your community.
- The builders who construct your home handle the difficult tasks
- The plumbers and electricians who lay down the pipes correctly for the hot water you enjoy daily and wire your house properly to supply light
- The sales clerk behind the counter assisting you with your purchase
- The bus driver responsible for getting you around during your day
- The pilot whose duty makes it possible for you to make distant travels easily and on time
- The mailman who has been around for as long as you can remember, bringing you mail
- The police, who work tirelessly to keep you safe
- The nurse and doctors working round the clock to be on standby for your health needs
- The crossing guards who ensure your children get across the road safely
- The volunteers, coaches, and referees of your kid's sports games
- The frequently anonymous faces of waiters and servers who serve you every day

The similarity between these individuals is how they go unnoticed, even though they are an intricate part of your day. They go about their day just like you without receiving the gratitude they deserve.

Understanding the Need of Channeling Your Gratitude to Strangers

One thing is certain, a halt in their work will greatly influence your day. Imagine stopping at your favorite coffee shop on your way to work only to realize they are not open. This singular disruption in your daily activity can greatly affect you, becoming a ripple effect on your day going forward.

These individuals give themselves daily to serve you, maybe not directly, but you receive their service. If you do not say a heartfelt thank you to them, you are not displaying gratitude. Some people do not see the need to appreciate these important strangers because they think they are just doing their job and are getting paid for it. It is their job, but their presence makes it easier for you to go about your day. By carrying out their task daily, you get to do yours without worrying about certain things, which makes them worthy of your gratitude.

How to Go About Extending Gratitude to Strangers

Today, pause and reflect on the assistance and contributions of these strangers in making your day. You might never get the chance to know them personally, but their efforts profoundly affect your life. They help you make your daily routines easier; because of them, you have more pleasant environments and safer communities. When you acknowledge their role in helping you improve your day and express it, you cultivate deeper appreciation, uplifting their spirits. Uplifting their spirits will help them go about their day more joyfully.

Intentionally and consciously, thank the individuals you encounter who assist you throughout your day. If you're in a shop, take the time to offer thanks in passing and genuine and heartfelt thanks to the person behind the counter who helped you locate things in the shop and everybody who helped you while you were there. Look them in the eye, smile sincerely, and express your gratitude for their help and service. When you recognize their effort genuinely, you make them feel valued. Also, it will help you establish a positive bond and connection with the other person. This simple act of gratitude will be one of the random acts of kindness they will remember for a long time, far, long after you've left the store. The exact words might not stick, but how you made them feel will not leave them in a hurry. Your gratitude will inspire them to continue providing excellent service to others.

When you're at a restaurant or cafe, show gratitude by appreciating everyone who serves you. Whether all they did was wipe the table, bring you the menu, serve your order, fill, and refill your glass, clear your table, or serve you the bill, remember to thank them every one every time and do it genuinely.

When walking your children to school, pay attention to the individuals who tend the crossings. These dedicated individuals are crucial in keeping your children safe while navigating the streets. You are not always there, but they are. Take a moment to sincerely thank them for their dedication and commitment to ensuring the well-being of your little ones. A simple thank you and a warm smile can go a long way in brightening their day and reinforcing their sense of purpose. Other strangers you should appreciate involving your children are their swimming instructors, teachers, and extracurricular tutors at their ballet, basketball, baseball, hockey, piano, football, or cooking classes.

Also, appreciate and show gratitude to the people at the airport. When traveling by plane, remember to thank important strangers and the loving individuals responsible for checking you in, security personnel, the person who goes through your documents as you board, and the cabin crew who welcome you as you board the plane. Remember to thank the personnel who help you while on the plane, from serving you food and drinks to providing information about your flight. It's normal to get a thank you from the flight crew, the pilot, the attendants, and the airline. It wouldn't be too much to return the favor because they made your life a little easier. Offering gratitude and appreciation will help them feel appreciated, valued, respected, and loved. So, remember to say "thank you" the next time you have to fly, from your onboarding, in the air and when you land.

Another set of strangers, short on your gratitude, are those we speak to over the phone. When you interact with people over the phone for business or other purposes, genuinely thank the person who assisted you through the entire process. It could be a sales rep, a customer care assistant, or a secretary of a company you are doing business with. Even on days when you feel frustrated because things do not go your way, which is perfectly normal, do not take it out on the individual on the other end of the phone. If you're upset at the call's outcome or dissatisfied with the service, do not take it out on them, they are only doing their jobs. They might not be personally responsible for the hurdle you encountered or your experience. In these situations, take a deep breath, count to three, then let go of your frustration and thank them for their effort in trying to help. Acknowledging and expressing your gratitude for their effort and hard work creates a more positive and productive interaction despite the outcome.

Strangers Not Worth Your Gratitude

There will be days when you encounter a stranger in service who is rude and without courtesy. However, it does not mean you react in a like manner toward them. Merely because they were not polite or did not accord you the respect required doesn't stop you from responding positively. You must not forget many are going through many trials and hardships, and a little kindness as gratitude is all they need to warm their hearts. Being grateful in these situations might be difficult, but you must not hinge your gratitude on the behaviors or actions of others. Something might have happened for them to react this way, or they might be struggling with something you will never know about. Treat everyone with the same level of love, compassion, and gratitude, regardless of their standing or actions.

Throughout the day, challenge yourself to thank as many people as possible while looking them in the eye and offering a warm smile. Whether the delivery person who brings a package to your door, the barista who prepares your morning coffee, or the janitor who keeps your workplace clean, take a moment to acknowledge their contributions. Recognize their hard work and let them know their efforts are seen and appreciated. When you do, don't just say thank you. Let them know it is indeed heartfelt. Rather than just saying "Thank you," say, "Thank you for helping me clean my office." "Thank you for preparing my coffee how I like it." "Thank you for driving me around today." "Thank you for the meal. It was delicious." Let them know how grateful you are. Emphasizing what you are grateful for is always more impactful for them and you.

By consciously expressing gratitude to the strangers in the street, you brighten their day and foster a culture of appreciation and kindness. Your gratitude has a ripple effect, inspiring others to pay it forward and creating a more compassionate society. Remember, every act of gratitude, no matter how small, has the power to make a significant difference in the lives of others.

As you conclude your day, take a moment to reflect on the encounters you had and the gratitude you expressed. Consider how it made you feel and the impact it might have had on the recipients. Allow yourself to bask in the warmth of gratitude as you embrace the knowledge that your words and actions contribute to a more compassionate and grateful world.

In a world where connection and kindness are often undervalued, expressing gratitude to strangers who contribute to your life is a powerful way to create a more harmonious and appreciative society. By extending your gratitude to those you will never know personally, you broaden your understanding of the interconnectedness of humanity and foster unity. As you approach the final day of this journey, remember to carry these lessons of gratitude with you beyond these fourteen days and continue to appreciate the people, things, and experiences in your lives, finding joy and fulfillment in the practice of gratitude. Remember, even the simplest acts of gratitude can transform lives - yours and the strangers on the street.

So, as you navigate the streets of life, pause, express your appreciation, and bring a smile to the strangers' faces who make a difference each day.

Remember to end your day with gratitude and keep smiling.

CHAPTER 14

Step 13 - Mistakes

Making mistakes is an inherent part of the human experience. Recognizing their value in your growth and embracing learning from your mistakes is crucial. Rather than dwelling on the errors, focusing on the lessons learned is more productive. Each mistake presents a unique chance to gain insight into yourself, your actions, and the consequences. Whether a small error in judgment or a significant misstep, mistakes provide valuable feedback to guide you toward making better choices.

Taking responsibility for your mistakes demonstrates maturity and integrity. It is acknowledging your role in the situation, accepting the consequences, and being accountable for your actions. Owning your mistakes creates an environment of honesty and trust within yourself and others. You will confront the situation's reality, learn from it, and take steps to rectify the harm caused or make amends.

While holding yourself accountable is essential, practicing self-compassion and avoiding harsh self-judgment is equally important. Making mistakes is a natural part of being human; everyone experiences them at various stages. Treat yourself with kindness and understanding rather than berating yourself for your shortcomings. This self-compassion helps cultivate a healthy mindset, allowing learning and growing from your mistakes without getting caught up in guilt or shame.

Guidance and support from trusted individuals give valuable insight and help navigate the aftermath of your mistakes. Trusted friends, family, mentors, or professionals can offer fresh perspectives, advice, and support during challenging times. They help you gain clarity, identify potential solutions, and encourage perseverance. Sharing your experiences with others who have faced similar challenges offers connection and reassurance, reminding you that you are not alone in your journey.

Using mistakes as motivation channels the lessons learned into positive action. Mistakes can be powerful catalysts for change and personal growth. They highlight areas requiring improvement, prompting setting new goals and inspiring you to strive for better outcomes. Instead of allowing mistakes to define you, view them as opportunities for transformation and progress. Each mistake becomes a stepping stone toward becoming a better version of yourself.

Additionally, learn from the mistakes of others. While gaining your experiences is essential, you can benefit from the wisdom and insights others share. Books, articles, podcasts, or conversations with people who experienced similar challenges give valuable lessons and strategies to avoid common pitfalls. Learning from others' experiences broadens your perspective and makes more informed decisions, potentially saving you from making the same mistakes.

Cultivating resilience is vital for dealing with mistakes. Mistakes can be discouraging, and setbacks can test your resolve. However, developing a resilient mindset enables you to bounce back from failures, setbacks, and mistakes. Resilience involves maintaining a positive attitude, adapting to changing circumstances, and staying committed to personal growth and goals. It allows you to view mistakes as temporary setbacks rather than permanent failures and empowers you to keep moving forward with determination and perseverance.

Making mistakes is an inevitable part of life, but how you respond matters. Embracing mistakes as learning opportunities, taking responsibility, practicing self-compassion, seeking guidance, using mistakes as motivation, learning from others, and cultivating resilience are essential steps in navigating and growing from mistakes. Adopting this mindset can transform mistakes into valuable lessons contributing to personal development, wisdom, and success.

Why Negativity Won't Help

Talking negatively about yourself or others has several detrimental effects. Engaging in negative self-talk, constantly self-criticizing, and self-belittling takes a toll on self-esteem and self-worth. The more you put yourself down, the more it reinforces a negative self-image, creating a toxic internal dialogue eroding self-confidence and inhibiting personal growth.

Furthermore, negative talk focuses on problems rather than solutions. Instead of seeking ways to overcome challenges, you get caught up in a negativity cycle keeping you stuck. It limits creative and constructive solutions to your issues. By dwelling on the negative aspects, you close yourself off to possibilities, hindering progress.

Negatively talking impacts relationships significantly. Constantly criticizing others or expressing negative opinions can strain relationships, creating a negative atmosphere and tension. People around you feel drained, uncomfortable, or defensive, damaging the trust and closeness in your interactions. Conversely, engaging in positive and supportive communication fosters healthier connections, promotes understanding, and builds stronger bonds.

Moreover, negative talk amplifies stress and anxiety. When constantly focused on what's wrong, worrying about potential outcomes, or indulging in self-deprecating thoughts, you perpetuate a negative emotional state. This increased stress and anxiety have detrimental effects on mental and physical well-being, impacting the overall quality of life.

Negative talk hampers motivation and progress. Constantly berating yourself or expressing pessimistic views undermines your belief in your abilities and limits your growth potential. It creates a sense of helplessness, making you feel stuck or incapable of achieving your goals. On the other hand, positive self-talk boosts motivation and resilience, fostering a belief to overcome challenges and progress.

Negatively talking influences your overall outlook on life. Constant negativity narrows perspective, making it difficult to see opportunities, solutions, or potential for growth. It creates a pessimistic lens through which you view the world, hindering your ability to appreciate the positive aspects of life and limiting your capacity for joy and fulfillment. Over time, keeping these negative thoughts in your mind and persistently sticking by them will only worsen matters. These thoughts will push you into a mindset where you will develop anxiety, stress, and mental health conditions like depression.

Lastly, negative talk affects how others perceive you. Consistently criticizing or speaking negatively about others reflects poorly on your character and influences how people perceive you. It can damage relationships, undermine trust, and create a negative reputation. Focusing on the positive qualities in others and engaging in constructive communication can enhance interactions, foster a positive environment, and contribute to healthier relationships.

Negatively talking has a range of detrimental effects. It damages self-esteem, limits problem-solving abilities, strains relationships, amplifies stress and anxiety, hampers motivation and progress, influences your overall outlook on life, and affects how others perceive you. In contrast, positive self-talk and fostering constructive communication empowers you, enhance well-being, and contribute to personal growth, healthier relationships, and a more positive and fulfilling life.

Learning from Mistakes

When encountering mistakes shifting your mindset away from negativity and embracing them as valuable learning opportunities is essential. Instead of dwelling on the negative aspects of your errors, focus on understanding where you went wrong and how to avoid making the same mistake again.

Reflecting on past errors allows you to delve deeper into the circumstances and factors contributing to the mistake. By examining the root causes, you gain insights into decision-making, underlying biases, or gaps in knowledge or skills. This self-reflection helps identify specific areas for improvement and provides a roadmap for growth.

Learning from mistakes enhances problem-solving abilities. Analyzing your errors, you gain a clearer understanding of the consequences and can identify alternative paths or actions that could have led to a more favorable outcome. This analytical thinking and introspection develop critical thinking skills, enabling you to approach future challenges with greater foresight and resilience.

Furthermore, mistakes can lead to innovation and creativity. When things don't go as planned, it forces you to think outside the box and consider alternative solutions. Mistakes often uncover unexplored possibilities or reveal unconventional approaches that could yield better results. Hence, embracing mistakes as learning opportunities encourages exploring different perspectives, experimenting with new ideas, and discovering innovative ways of tackling problems.

In addition, mistakes can be humbling experiences fostering personal growth and empathy. You confront your fallibility and recognize that everyone is prone to errors when making mistakes. This realization can cultivate empathy and understanding as you become more compassionate toward others when they make mistakes. It creates an environment of openness and support, where learning and growth are valued over judgment and criticism.

Reflecting on past mistakes fuels a lifelong pursuit of knowledge and improvement. Each error becomes a stepping stone toward acquiring new skills, expanding your knowledge base, and seeking continuous learning opportunities. It motivates seeking guidance from experts, mentors, or educational resources, further enhancing personal and professional development.

Moreover, mistakes provide valuable feedback helping refine your goals and redefine success. Understanding where you went wrong can redefine your strategies and set realistic expectations. This adaptive approach allows you to make more informed decisions and align your efforts with your desired outcomes. If you fail to maintain this approach, moving forward and growing from problems won't be possible.

Embracing mistakes as learning opportunities is crucial for personal growth and development. Reflecting on errors helps you understand their root causes, improve decision-making, and enhance problem-solving skills. Mistakes foster innovation, creativity, empathy, and a lifelong commitment to learning. By shifting your perspective and focusing on the lessons gained from mistakes, you can turn setbacks into stepping stones toward greater success and fulfillment.

Perhaps you were given a leadership opportunity at work. However, due to a lack of effective communication and delegation, the project you were leading did not meet the desired outcome. The mistake was not adequately communicating expectations to your team members or delegating tasks effectively, resulting in missed deadlines and subpar deliverables.

What You Learned

This mistake taught you the importance of clear communication and delegation in leadership roles. You realized effective communication involves setting clear expectations, providing necessary information, and actively listening to your team members. You learned that proper delegation means assigning tasks based on team members' strengths, providing support and guidance, and monitoring progress.

What Good Came from It?

While the mistake perhaps had immediate negative consequences, several positive outcomes emerged from it, such as:

Improved communication: The mistake prompted you to become more mindful of your communication style and take steps to enhance it. You became more proactive in clarifying expectations, ensuring everyone is on the same page, and actively seeking feedback to foster better communication within your team. Your team won't face setbacks as these effective communication channels will facilitate the delivery of relevant information.

Enhanced delegation skills: Recognizing the importance of delegation, you took the opportunity to develop better delegation techniques. You learned to assess team members' skills and allocate tasks, accordingly, provide necessary resources and guidance, and establish a system for tracking progress and offering support.

Strengthened relationships: You built stronger relationships with your team members through open and transparent communication. By acknowledging your mistake, taking responsibility, and seeking input from your team, you demonstrated humility and a willingness to learn. It fostered trust, collaboration, and shared responsibility within the team.

Professional growth: The mistake provided a valuable learning experience contributing to your professional growth. You demonstrated self-awareness and a commitment to personal development by acknowledging the areas where you fell short. You actively sought resources, training, or mentoring to improve your leadership skills, ultimately enhancing leadership effectiveness.

Resilience and adaptability: The mistake taught you the importance of resilience and adaptability in the face of setbacks. It helped you develop the ability to bounce back from failures, learn from them, and adjust your approach to future projects. This resilience and adaptability are transferable skills benefiting various aspects of your life.

By reflecting on the mistake, learning from it, and taking positive action, you turned the setback into an opportunity for growth and improvement. This example illustrates how mistakes can lead to valuable insight, personal development, stronger relationships, and enhanced leadership skills. Life is full of examples where you make the wrong move and fall apart. Surprisingly, your mistakes are a chance to identify the root cause, address the situation accordingly, and learn from these setbacks for a brighter future.

Ending the day with gratitude and a positive attitude can be a powerful practice. Reflecting on what you are grateful for helps shift your focus toward the positive aspects of your life, fostering contentment and well-being. It helps you maintain a positive mindset and approach challenges with resilience and optimism. So, take a moment to appreciate the lessons learned from mistakes, express gratitude for growth opportunities, and end your day with a smile, knowing that each experience contributes to your personal and professional development.

Remember to end your day with gratitude and keep smiling.

CHAPTER 15

Step 14 – Yourself

You've probably heard people say how you should be grateful for all your blessings. Usually, blessings include your family, your job, the people around you, and the opportunities you've been given. Yet, rarely have you been told to be thankful for yourself, the person you are on the inside, and the great qualities you bring to the table. It does not mean the other blessings - the loving and supportive people around you or incredible opportunities - hold less value. However, when you understand your worth and are grateful for yourself, only then will you fully practice gratitude. Once you make yourself the focal point of gratitude, you'll notice tremendous changes in your personality and life.

By now, you've learned several gratitude practices, starting with your gratitude list at the beginning of each day, followed by practicing gratitude multiple times a day. As a result, you have noticed quite a difference in your outlook. If you've been following these tips and are consistent with your gratitude practice, you must feel much happier and more fulfilled in your life. When you take a few moments every day to focus on the good in your life, you'll reap the rewards of a happier life.

This final chapter teaches you about the power of self-gratitude. While you might find it incredibly easy and refreshing to be grateful for and to your loved ones, friends, and others, it might be hard to be grateful for yourself. Appreciating others usually comes naturally to many. However, appreciating yourself is another subject.

As you're consistently navigating the journey of self-discovery, it might not be easy to like yourself, let alone appreciate yourself. However, self-gratitude can help you do both simultaneously. When you practice self-gratitude, you become more confident, and self-esteem develops immensely. Once you turn the practice of gratitude on its head and make it about you, your gratitude practice will increase a hundredfold. As Rhonda Bryne said, "Unless you fill yourself up first, you have nothing to give anybody." If you don't love and appreciate yourself, how can you do the same for others?

Sometimes, you're your own worst critic, finding flaws in every aspect of your personality. Typically, you blame yourself for many things that aren't your fault. You wouldn't judge them the same way if it were another person. So, why not show yourself the same kindness? When you practice gratitude, it becomes impossible to be negative. So, when you direct this gratitude toward yourself, you'll have a hard time picking out flaws and treating yourself unkindly. Therefore, practicing self-gratitude is as equally important as your regular gratitude practice. Furthermore, the benefits are great, if not better. You not only feel less stressed and more confident but also be smiling more often, generally feeling better, and enjoying the blessings of this life with love in your heart.

Self-Gratitude and Kindness

Self-gratitude can be defined as affirming and appreciating things about yourself you admire, including your personality traits, looks, abilities, talents, skills, knowledge, style, and choices. The world is full of negativity; if you're not careful and allow it to get to you, it will become the predominant voice in your head. Your self-esteem will deteriorate faster than you realize once you listen to that self-hating, pessimistic, critical voice. Instead of accepting reality, this negative voice will point out every flaw you apparently have, everything you don't like about yourself, and what you should be doing better. There's nothing wrong with striving for more, but you should be content with what you have while you work on yourself. Negative self-talk has never helped anyone; it limits your dreams and ambitions. This behavior will do nothing but restrict your abilities and make you doubt your self-worth.

Conversely, self-gratitude can spur you into action and make you believe in yourself. You see yourself in a new light when you appreciate all you have to offer. Your confidence will dramatically improve, and you'll feel valued by others and yourself. Some have the misconception that self-gratitude can make them seem narcissistic. However, this couldn't be further from the truth. Self-gratitude is about knowing you're worth something but not trying to prove it to others, which is narcissism. As you practice self-gratitude, you see a completely different side of yourself and grow even further as a person.

How to Add Self-Gratitude to Your Daily Life

You can practice self-gratitude throughout the day in many ways. These simple yet effective activities will make you believe in your abilities and help you see yourself as someone worth something.

1. Use Daily Affirmations

Like your gratitude list or affirmations, you can practice self-gratitude affirmations daily. These affirmations will make you feel better about yourself because they focus on the good you bring to this world as a person and how the world would be a little less if you weren't in it. You can incorporate these positive affirmations into your schedule in many ways:

You can make self-affirmation cards like the affirmation cards and gratitude flashcards you created for gratitude focus points during the day. Print or handwrite them and put them in places where you will see them. For instance, you can put them on your bathroom mirror, car, study, or work desk, or even stick them on the fridge.

- Read the affirmations out loud while you look at yourself in the mirror. Tell yourself these are facts and shut out the negative voices in your mind.
- Write down self-love affirmations in a notebook or journal, and keep it by your bed. Write at least one affirmation before you wake up and one before bed.

2. Start Journaling

Journaling is a very healthy habit, and like you learned to practice gratitude journaling, incorporate self-gratitude prompts into your journal entries. Take extra time to write your journal entry instead of focusing on your to-do list for the day. Write down a few things you like, or love, about yourself at least once a day. Here are some prompts you can use:

- I'm at my best when I... and I absolutely love this about myself because it lets me...
- I'm really good at... and I love it because...
- I feel great about my appearance. My favorite thing about my body is...
- I don't know anyone else who can...
- I think I'm special because...
- I feel confident and happy when I ... because it shows my ability to ......
- I am grateful for my strong sense of ...... because it helps me navigate and understand ......

- I love that I possess the ..... quality because it allows me to connect with others deeper
- My favorite aspect of my personality is my ...... because it brings ......
- I am proud of myself for handling ....with grace and resilience

3. Compliment Yourself

When was the last time someone gave you a compliment? How did it feel? For most people, it feels amazing. For others, it's hard to believe. You don't have to wait for someone else to compliment you when you know yourself better than anyone. Compliment yourself on one thing every day before you leave for work to stop your negative self-talk. For instance, you could compliment:

- How you look
- Your beautiful smile
- Your hairstyle
- Getting the kids ready and out the door on time
- Prepping lunches the night before
- Keeping up with laundry and housework
- Doing life even when you're not in the mood
- Taking on new challenges and trying something different

The list can go on and on. You can do many commendable things if you focus on the positives instead of the negatives. Don't think about what you couldn't do or don't have, but the opposite. Compliment yourself. At first, it might seem awkward or weird, but you'll be surprised at how good it makes you feel after a while.

4. Be Specific

Like you learned to be specific about your gratitude statements, self-gratitude also requires you to be specific when you list the things about yourself, you're grateful for. Remove the broad, generic sentences, and include statements specific to your exact qualities. Consider these examples:

- Instead of saying, *"My outfit looks great today."* You can say, *"I love the way my pants complement my top. I'm a good stylist."*
- Rather than saying, *"I like my hairstyle."* You could say, *"I love how my bangs complement my face and make my eyes look beautiful."*
- Instead of thinking, *"I'm glad I got my kids to school on time."* You should think, *"I'm thankful I had the foresight to plan ahead and prepare the lunches last night to get my kids to school on time. I'm a good planner."*

The more specific your statements, the better you'll appreciate yourself without feeling redundant and dull.

5. Notice Your Qualities

Your qualities are what make you unique and appreciable. When you notice specific qualities about yourself, you can practice self-gratitude and highlight these good traits, bringing them to your attention. For instance, are you a special kind person? Maybe you're more empathetic than most people. Or maybe you're a helper and jump at the chance to help those in need. Notice the qualities that make up your personality, and soon you'll realize you have admirable qualities deserving of appreciation. Be specific about these qualities. Instead of saying, "I'm a nice person," you should point out the specific reason you believe this quality. Like, "I was kind to the new kid in school when others were bullying him."

6. Write Down Compliments You Receive

Usually, when someone gets a compliment, they say thank you and move on with their day. Instead of acknowledging the compliment, you forget about it. So, when you get a compliment, whether about your outfit, personality, abilities, or anything else, pause for a moment and genuinely thank the person who gave the compliment. When you get a chance, write down the compliment you received in your journal or a notebook. When you write down what was said, you'll remember how you felt, and later when you feel down, read these compliments from your loved ones, acquaintances, and even strangers, and your heart will truly be happy. You might discover qualities about yourself you weren't aware of, and now you'll have something new to be grateful for.

7. Notice Something New

It's easy to take good things about your life for granted, and your own self is no exception. You might feel your qualities are redundant, nothing out of the ordinary, or something to be valued. However, when you find new things about yourself every day, things you appreciate, you'll consistently practice self-gratitude. You'll be surprised at the new things you can appreciate about yourself, from how you look to a problem you solved at work. Take a minute every day to write down what you noticed, and soon you'll have a long list of good qualities about yourself.

Self-Gratitude Affirmations

A great way to start your self-gratitude process is to immerse yourself in quotes and affirmations highlighting your positive attributes.

Here are a few to kickstart your journey:

"I am grateful for my ability to perceive solutions to everyday challenges."

Once you recognize your problem-solving abilities, you appreciate how remarkable you truly are. Whether you excel at seeing the big picture, paying attention to details, or tackling problems head-on, you should discover and celebrate your unique strengths.

"I am thankful for my strength and resilience, knowing I have the power to overcome."

During tough times, it's essential to acknowledge your inner strength. Even if you don't feel particularly strong, continuing to face each day and manage daily stresses and responsibilities demonstrates strength surpassing your perceptions.

"I am grateful for my positive outlook, embracing pleasant and difficult moments as valuable experiences."

If you possess a positive, optimistic attitude, rejoice, and take pride in your ability to view each day, regardless of its ups and downs, as an integral part of your growth journey. Your mindset and willingness to learn from circumstances contribute to your development as an individual.

"I'm glad I had the opportunity to know Sarah. She played a significant role in improving my friendship skills."

When you experience losing loved ones, appreciating the positive aspects of those relationships amid the pain is challenging. Celebrate your friendships and connections by reflecting on each person's impact on your life. Did Sarah help you become a better friend? Did she impart valuable lessons or wisdom? Recognizing the influence of others showcases grief and gratitude after a loss.

"I appreciate my unwavering thirst for knowledge, personal growth, and self-improvement."

What makes you unique? Do you revel in acquiring new skills or knowledge? Do you constantly push yourself to achieve greater heights in sports or professional endeavors? Take a moment to celebrate your distinctive aspects by acknowledging and appreciating them.

Practicing self-gratitude helps you recognize yourself for who you truly are and your worth. You learn to appreciate the unique qualities that make you "you." When you focus on what you love about yourself, you are less vulnerable to negative self-talk, and your confidence grows daily. So, take a moment of your time to celebrate yourself today, along with all the other blessings in your life.

Remember to end your day with gratitude and keep smiling.

Conclusion

"Gratitude can transform common days into thanksgivings, turn routine jobs into joy, and change ordinary opportunities into blessings."
- William Arthur Ward

This wonderful quote captures the essence of what it's like to practice gratitude. It's a transformative practice changing your life tremendously. Has this book truly resonated with you, reminding you of the immense value gratitude holds in your life? If it is challenging to incorporate the exercises in this book into your routine, that's perfectly okay. The beauty of this book is its flexibility. You choose the exercises that best fit your lifestyle and your availability. Whether you decide to try them all or select a few favorites, taking that first step toward a more grateful life is what truly matters.

Practicing gratitude is not a one-time activity; it's a continuous process unfolding over time. It's like tending a garden - nurturing the seeds of gratitude and watching them grow, blossom, and transform lives. Each day, as you make a conscious effort to express gratitude, you shift your focus from what's lacking to what's already present, from problems to possibilities, and from despair to hope. Consider starting your day with a gratitude ritual that resonates with you. It could be as simple as reflecting on three things you're grateful for or jotting them down in a journal. This way, you set a positive tone for hours ahead, inviting more blessings into your life and cultivating an abundant mindset.

Similarly, ending your day on a grateful note can bring peace and contentment. Take a few moments to reflect on the day's blessings, acknowledging the small victories, acts of kindness, and moments of joy. This practice helps you appreciate the gifts of the present and ensures you go to sleep with a heart filled with gratitude. Remember, gratitude is a powerful practice touching every aspect of your life. It opens your eyes to the beauty in the ordinary, helps you recognize the support of loved ones, and deepens your connection with the world around you. It's not about waiting for big achievements or grand gestures but appreciating the little things that make life extraordinary.

So, be encouraged to keep practicing gratitude, allowing it to weave its magic into your daily existence. Let it be your constant companion as it accompanies you through life's ups and downs and reminds you of the precious moments that often go unnoticed. As you close this book and continue your journey, always remember that gratitude has the power to transform your life. Gratitude has the remarkable ability to reframe your experiences. It allows you to see the silver linings in challenging situations, to find lessons in failures, and to appreciate growth from adversity. It's the first step toward making your days brighter, your heart lighter, and your world more joyful.

References

(N.d.). Choosingtherapy.com. https://www.choosingtherapy.com/how-to-practice-gratitude/

(N.d.). Indeed.com. https://ca.indeed.com/career-advice/career-development/benefits-of-job

(N.d.). Masterclass.com. https://www.masterclass.com/articles/making-a-mistake

10 benefits of having a job. (n.d.). Jobcluster.com. https://www.jobcluster.com/career-advice/10-benefits-of-having-a-job-56

10 easy ways to practice self-gratitude - MY BIG IDEA. (n.d.). https://mbimybigidea.com/2021/05/28/10-easy-ways-to-practice-self-gratitude/

13 things I've learned writing 1,024 gratitude lists. (2018, July 13). Chris Winfield. https://www.chriswinfield.com/gratitude-lists/

17 reasons I am grateful for my husband. (2018, May 25). Blackandmarriedwithkids.com. https://blackandmarriedwithkids.com/17-reasons-i-am-grateful-for-my-husband/

4 Reasons To Be Thankful For Your Health. (n.d.). Full Spectrum Emergency Room and Urgent Care. https://www.fullspectrumer.com/blog/2021/november/4-reasons-to-be-thankful-for-your-health/

5 reasons why your career is important in life. (n.d.). Findfulfillingwork.org. https://www.findfulfillingwork.org/blog/why-your-career-is-so-important-in-life

7 Things to be Thankful for in Your Job (even if it's the wrong job). (2018, November 21). ALRA | Australia's Leading Recruitment Agency. https://alra.com.au/7-things-to-be-thankful-for-in-your-job/

Applebury, G. (2021, April 23). Thank you, family: 100+ messages that glow with gratitude. LoveToKnow. https://www.lovetoknow.com/quotes-quips/relationships/thank-you-family-100-messages-that-glow-gratitude

Arlin Cuncic, M. A. (2015, February 27). 6 friendship benefits: Why it's important to stay close to your friends. Verywell Mind. https://www.verywellmind.com/the-importance-of-friendship-3024371

Barkley, S. (2022, December 9). Why are friendships important? 9 health benefits. Psych Central. https://psychcentral.com/relationships/benefits-of-friendship

Beau, A. (2020, November 21). How I made self-gratitude a habit (and stopped feeling awkward about it). Shine. https://advice.theshineapp.com/articles/how-i-made-self-gratitude-a-habit-and-stopped-feeling-awkward-about-it/

Benedict, F. (2019, November 20). 4 reasons to be thankful for your family this Thanksgiving. Chopra. https://chopra.com/articles/4-reasons-to-be-thankful-for-your-family-this-thanksgiving

Berliet, M. (2016, March 14). 47 really good reasons to thank the person you love right this second. Thought Catalog. https://thoughtcatalog.com/melanie-berliet/2016/03/47-simple-reasons-to-thank-the-person-you-love-right-this-second/

Blencowe, I. (2020, August 11). A Complete Guide to Gratitude Journaling and Why it's More Important Than Ever. In Fitness And In Health. https://medium.com/in-fitness-and-in-health/the-complete-guide-to-gratitude-journaling-and-why-its-more-important-than-ever-cb38271f58a

Books, J. P. (2023, March 11). Benefits of Keeping a Gratitude List: Cultivate a positive mindset. Just Plan Books. https://justplanbooks.co.uk/benefits-of-keeping-a-gratitude-list/

Boynton, E. (2022, April 11). Taking breaks is good for your brain — here's why. Right as Rain by UW Medicine. https://rightasrain.uwmedicine.org/mind/well-being/taking-breaks

Brickel, R. E. (2017, March 2). Healthy relationships matter more than we think. PsychAlive. https://www.psychalive.org/healthy-relationships-matter/

Byrne, R. (2012). The Magic. Simon & Schuster. https://books.google.at/books?id=Fz2qe7V2TgUC

Byrne, R. (2012). The Magic. Simon & Schuster. https://books.google.at/books?id=Fz2qe7V2TgUC

Cantore, N. (2017, November 27). 8 reasons why I'm grateful for my family. The Odyssey Online. https://www.theodysseyonline.com/8-reasons-why-im-grateful-for-my-family

CarePro Health Services. (n.d.). 5 Reasons to Be Thankful For Your Health. Careprohs.Com. https://www.careprohs.com/blog/post/5-reasons-to-be-thankful-for-your-health

Chernoff, A. (2014, August 7). 40 things we forget to thank our best friends for. Marc and Angel Hack Life. https://www.marcandangel.com/2014/08/06/40-things-we-forget-to-thank-our-best-friends-for/

Coelho, S. (2011, January 20). Can't stop thinking about past mistakes? This may be why. Psych Central. https://psychcentral.com/blog/how-to-stop-ruminating-on-the-past

Courtney E. Ackerman, M. A. (2017, April 19). Gratitude journal: 66 templates & ideas for daily journaling. Positivepsychology.com. https://positivepsychology.com/gratitude-journal/

Darcy Eikenberg, P. C. C. (2022, November 15). 6 things to be thankful for at work (& 3 will surprise you). Red Cape Revolution with Coach Darcy Eikenberg; RedCapeRevolution.com. https://redcaperevolution.com/6-things-to-be-thankful-for-at-work/

Davenport, B. (2022, August 29). How to create A gratitude list and make it A habit. Mindful Zen. https://mindfulzen.co/gratitude-list/

Davis, A. (2021, October 30). Need a break from life? Here's how and when to do it. Ambitiously Alexa. https://ambitiouslyalexa.com/how-to-take-a-break-from-life/

Davis, J. M. (1641389009000). It's time to be grateful for work it's a good thing to have. Linkedin.com. https://www.linkedin.com/pulse/its-time-grateful-work-good-thing-have-janeane-m-davis-j-d-/

Davis, S. (2020, February 29). Thank you, next? 5 things to say "thank you" for to your ex before starting A new relationship. YourTango. https://www.yourtango.com/2020331960/thank-you-next-being-grateful-ex-new-relationship

Deitz, B. (2015, November 6). 8 reasons to be more grateful for your partner. Bustle. https://www.bustle.com/articles/121973-8-reasons-to-be-more-grateful-for-your-partner-right-now

Deschene, L. (2015, March 12). 40 ways to give yourself a break. Tiny Buddha. https://tinybuddha.com/blog/40-ways-to-give-yourself-a-break/

Dixon, J. A. (2022, January 9). What is a gratitude list, and how do you use them? Youth Employment UK. https://www.youthemployment.org.uk/what-is-a-gratitude-list-2/

Doegar, A. (2022, January 27). Top 5 personal & psychological benefits of A job in A person's life. India's Largest Online Career Acceleration Platform. https://www.expertrons.com/blog/emotional-benefits-of-a-job/

Elaine Houston, B. S. (2019, April 9). How to express gratitude to others: 19 examples & ideas. Positivepsychology.com. https://positivepsychology.com/how-to-express-gratitude/

Elmore, R. (2021, October 28). How to Say Thank You to a FriendHaving great friends is one of the many joys in life. Your friends are alwa. SimplyNoted. https://simplynoted.com/blogs/news/15-ways-thank-you-being-friend

Finding happiness with nature. (n.d.). Live Happy. https://www.livehappy.com/science/finding-happiness-with-nature

Gallo, A. (2010, April 28). You've made A mistake. Now what? Harvard Business Review. https://hbr.org/2010/04/youve-made-a-mistake-now-what

Gratitude. (n.d.). Psychology Today. https://www.psychologytoday.com/us/basics/gratitude

Gravier, E. (2019, July 2). Spending 2 hours in nature each week can make you happier and healthier, a new study says. CNBC. https://www.cnbc.com/amp/2019/07/02/spending-2-hours-in-nature-per-week-can-make-you-happier-and-healthier.html

Healthdirect Australia. (2022). Building and maintaining healthy relationships. https://www.healthdirect.gov.au/building-and-maintaining-healthy-relationships

Hiregy. (2021, November 17). Job thankfulness and overall happiness: 8 reasons to be thankful. Hiregy. https://www.hiregy.com/job-thankfulness-and-overall-happiness-8-reasons-to-be-thankful/

How nature can make you kinder, happier, and more creative. (n.d.). Greater Good. https://greatergood.berkeley.edu/article/item/how_nature_makes_you_kinder_happier_more_creative

How to be more grateful. (n.d.). Headspace. https://www.headspace.com/articles/how-to-be-more-grateful

How to express gratitude. (2017, July 17). Psych Central. https://psychcentral.com/health/ways-to-express-gratitude

How to practice gratitude and increase your happiness. (2020, January 6). Pine Rest. https://www.pinerest.org/newsroom/articles/practice-gratitude-increase-happiness-blog/

https://www.jakeshell.com/v/s/www.jakeshell.com/articles/2018/12/17/gratitude?amp_gsa=1&amp_js_v=a9&format=amp&usqp=mq331AQIUAKwASCAAgM%3D

Intelligent Change. (2017, May 17). The ultimate gratitude journal guide. Intelligent Change. https://www.intelligentchange.com/blogs/read/ultimate-gratitude-journal-guide

Johnson, M. (2021, April 19). Avoid these 3 common mistakes when you write a gratitude list. YouAlignedTM. https://youaligned.com/lifestyle/gratitude-list-dos-and-donts/

Johnson, S., & BA. (2022, April 25). What is self-gratitude and how can you practice it? Joincake.com. https://www.joincake.com/blog/self-gratitude/

Kalaf, J. (2021). Benefits of gratitude: How gratitude changes you and your brain: 5 ways to develop an attitude of gratitude. Independently Published.

Lebow, H. I. (2017, November 5). Mindfulness & gratitude: Why and how they should pair. Psych Central. https://psychcentral.com/blog/how-gratitude-and-mindfulness-go-hand-in-hand

Marielle. (2020, November 4). 15 simple ways to practice gratitude as a family. Lovin' Life with Littles. https://lovinlifewithlittles.com/15-simple-ways-to-practice-gratitude-as-a-family/

Martinez, L. (2018, November 15). Gratitude for self. HEART in Mind. https://loreamartinez.com/2018/11/15/gratitude-for-self/

MindTools. (n.d.). Mindtools.com. https://www.mindtools.com/a27yhpa/how-to-learn-from-your-mistakes

Mitchell, M. (1570119530000). Reasons to be thankful for your job (even when you don't feel thankful at all). Linkedin.com. https://www.linkedin.com/pulse/reasons-thankful-your-job-even-when-you-dont-feel-all-melanie/

Morin, A. (2014, November 23). 7 scientifically proven benefits of gratitude that will motivate you to give thanks year-round. Forbes. https://www.forbes.com/sites/amymorin/2014/11/23/7-scientifically-proven-benefits-of-gratitude-that-will-motivate-you-to-give-thanks-year-round/?sh=552fd483183c

Morin, A. (2017, July 17). 5 ways to turn your mistake into A valuable life lesson. Forbes. https://www.forbes.com/sites/amymorin/2017/07/17/5-ways-to-turn-your-mistake-into-a-valuable-life-lesson/?sh=b9859011c01f

MummyConstant. (2017, October 25). 5 Reasons to be thankful for family. MummyConstant. https://mummyconstant.com/5-reasons-thankful-family/

Nollan, J. (2020, June 30). How to take A break from life and everything if you really need one. A Conscious Rethink. https://www.aconsciousrethink.com/13514/how-to-take-a-break-from-life/

Northwestern Medicine. (n.d.). 5 benefits of healthy relationships. Northwestern Medicine. https://www.nm.org/healthbeat/healthy-tips/5-benefits-of-healthy-relationships

Okerlund, R. (n.d.). 4 easy gratitude practices for families to start this fall (and continue all year long!). ParentMap. https://www.parentmap.com/article/easy-gratitude-practices-thanksgiving-empathy

Rebecca Joy Stanborough, M. F. A. (2020, September 18). 7 science-backed benefits of indoor plants. Healthline. https://www.healthline.com/health/healthy-home-guide/benefits-of-indoor-plants

Reid, S. (n.d.). Gratitude: The benefits and how to practice it - Helpguide. org. https://www.helpguide.org/articles/mental-health/gratitude.htm

Reily, M. (2016, October 17). 12 reasons to be thankful for family. The Odyssey Online. https://www.theodysseyonline. com/12-reasons-thankful-for-family

Salazar, M. (2018, July 31). Through thick and thin: 15 reasons to be thankful for your family. Blog | Nixplay. https://blog.nixplay. com/2018/07/through-thick-thin-15-reasons-thankful-family/

Scott, S. J. (2021, January 16). How to create a gratitude list: 6 steps to be more thankful in 2023. Develop Good Habits; S.J. Scott. https://www. developgoodhabits.com/gratitude-list/

Sharpe, R. (2022, June 9). Gratitude list: 200+ things to be grateful for. Declutter The Mind. https://declutterthemind.com/blog/gratitude-list/

Shellenberger, J. (2018, December 23). Why it is OK to be grateful for material things. Jakeshell.com; @JakeShell.

Shutterfly Community. (2018, July 3). How to start a gratitude journal you'll actually keep. Ideas & Inspiration; Shutterfly. https://www.shutterfly. com/ideas/how-to-start-a-gratitude-journal/

Shutterfly Community. (2019a, February 26). 100 things to be thankful for in your life. Ideas & Inspiration; Shutterfly. https://www.shutterfly.com/ ideas/things-to-be-thankful-for/

Sisson, M. (2014, November 27). What It Means to Be Thankful for Your Health. Mark's Daily Apple. https://www.marksdailyapple.com/what-it-means-to-be-thankful-for-your-health/

Smith, J. (2017, November 1). 4 Reasons to Be Thankful for Your Body (As It Is Today). MyFitnessPal Blog. https://blog.myfitnesspal.com/4-reasons-to-be-thankful-for-your-body-as-it-is-today/

StacyTR. (2022, April 19). Why family matters: I am thankful for my family because. Family Oriented. https://familyoriented.net/i-am-thankful-for-my-family-because/

Stallings, A. M. (2020, July 22). Complimenting strangers changed my life – you should give it a try. The Guardian. https://amp.theguardian.com/v/s/amp.theguardian.com/lifeandstyle/2020/jul/22/coronavirus-strangers-compliments-street-seattle?amp_gsa=1&amp_js_v=a9&usqp=mq331AQIUAKwASCAAgM%3D

Sustain Recovery. (2021, November 1). How gratitude can heal within families. Sustain Recovery - Adolescent Extended Care and Transitional Living. https://www.sustainrecovery.com/how-gratitude-can-heal-within-families/

Tewari, A. (2022, July 15). Self-appreciation: What it is & 7 ways to appreciate yourself. Gratitude - The Life Blog. https://blog.gratefulness.me/self-appreciation/

The Beatles – Eleanor Rigby. (n.d.). Genius. https://genius.com/The-beatles-eleanor-rigby-lyrics

Tierney, J. (2011, November 21). A serving of gratitude may save the day. The New York Times. https://www.nytimes.com/2011/11/22/science/a-serving-of-gratitude-brings-healthy-dividends.html

What causes negative thinking and how to stop it. (n.d.). Baptist Health. https://www.baptisthealth.com/blog/family-health/what-causes-negative-thinking-and-how-to-stop-it

What is gratitude? Definition, meaning & how to practice it (examples). (n.d.). Betterup.com. https://www.betterup.com/blog/gratitude-definition-how-to-practice

Willow, & Sage. (2019, November 28). 25 ways to show yourself gratitude. Willow and Sage Magazine. https://willowandsage.com/25-ways-to-show-yourself-gratitude/

Yang, S. (2019, August 7). 22 Reasons to Be Thankful for Your Body. The Thirty. https://thethirty.whowhatwear.com/reasons-to-be-thankful-for-your-body

高啟禎 J. K. (2022, November 19). Gratitude practices for the whole family. The Mom Edit. https://themomedit.com/momlife-on-life-family-gratitude-practice-thanksgiving-traditions-kids-books-mindfulness-activities-janice

Made in United States
Troutdale, OR
10/14/2023

13717019R00096